RISE, RED RIVER

ALSO BY TARA BEAGAN

Dreary and Izzy
Honour Beat
In Spirit
The Ministry of Grace
Reckoning (with Andy Moro)

RISE, RED RIVER

TARA BEAGAN

PLAYWRIGHTS CANADA PRESS
TORONTO

First edition: June 2025
Printed and bound in Canada by Imprimerie Gauvin Ltée, Gatineau

Jacket art and design by Jaime Black-Morsette
Author photo by Andy Moro

Playwrights Canada Press
202-269 Richmond St. W., Toronto, ON M5V 1X1
416.703.0013 | info@playwrightscanada.com | www.playwrightscanada.com

LIBRARY AND ARCHIVES CANADA CATALOGUING IN PUBLICATION
Title: Rise, Red River / Tara Beagan.
Names: Beagan, Tara, author.
Description: A play. | Text in English, French and Anishinaabemowin.
Identifiers: Canadiana (print) 2025011942OE | Canadiana (ebook) 20250119447E | ISBN 9780369105486 (softcover) | ISBN 9780369105493 (PDF) | ISBN 9780369105509 (EPUB)
Classification: LCC PS8603.E34 R57 2025 | DDC C812/.6—dc23

Titre: Rise, Red River / Tara Beagan.
Noms: Beagan, Tara, auteur.
Description: Pièce de théâtre. | Texte en anglais, en français et en anishinaabemowin.
Identifiants: Canadiana (livre imprimé) 2025011942OF | Canadiana (livre numérique) 20250119447F | ISBN 9780369105486 (couverture souple) | ISBN 9780369105493 (PDF) | ISBN 9780369105509 (EPUB)
Classification: LCC PS8603.E34 R57 2025 | CDD C812/.6—dc23

Playwrights Canada Press staff work across Turtle Island, on Treaty 13 and Treaty 20 territories, as well as unceded lands, which are the current, ancestral, and future homes of the Anishinaabe Nations (Ojibwe / Chippewa, Odawa, Potawatomi, Algonquin, Saulteaux, Nipissing, and Mississauga / Michi Saagiig), the Wendat, members of the Haudenosaunee Confederacy (Mohawk, Oneida, Onondaga, Cayuga, Seneca, and Tuscarora), and the xʷməθkʷəy̓əm (Musqueam), Sḵwx̱wú7mesh (Squamish), and səlilwətaɬ (Tsleil-Waututh) Nations, as well as Metis and Inuit peoples. It always was and always will be Indigenous land.

We acknowledge the financial support of the Canada Council for the Arts, the Ontario Arts Council (OAC), Ontario Creates, the Government of Ontario, and the Government of Canada for our publishing activities.

Canada Council for the Arts | Conseil des arts du Canada
ONTARIO ARTS COUNCIL
CONSEIL DES ARTS DE L'ONTARIO
an Ontario government agency
un organisme du gouvernement de l'Ontario
ONTARIO CREATES | ONTARIO CRÉATIF
Canada
Ontario

To all the fierce Indigenous matriarchs of Treaty 1. To the founders of Drag the Red and all the volunteers who persevere with courage and hope. You astound.

"They treat Mother Earth like they treat women . . . They think they can own us, buy us, sell us, trade us, rent us, poison us, rape us, destroy us, use us as entertainment and kill us."

« Ils traitent notre Mère-Terre de la même manière dont ils traitent les femmes . . . Ils s'imaginent qu'ils peuvent nous posséder, nous acheter, nous vendre, nous échanger, nous louer, nous empoisonner, nous violer, nous détruire, nous utiliser comme du divertissement et nous assassiner. »

"Odoodawaawaan ninge-aki daabishko nakake gaa-doodawaawaad ikwewag . . . Inendamoog ji-gashkitoowaad ji-dibenimigoowiyaang, ji-adaawewigowiyaang, ji-adaawaagewigowiyaang, ji-meshkwadoonigewiwiyaang, ji-diba'igegoowiyaang, ji-bichibooniwiwiyaang, ji-zhoonaabaji'igoowiyaang, ji-zhoonaachiji'igowiyaang, ji-aabajii'igowiyaang daabishkoo odaminwaagana' zhigo giga-nisigoomin."

—Lisa Brunner, Anishinaabe of White Earth Nation

FOREWORD
GENEVIÈVE PELLETIER & THOMAS MORGAN JONES

L'eau.

Tout commence avec l'eau.

Et s'il n'y avait plus d'eau.

Où est-ce qu'on commencerait?

La Femme.

Tout commence avec la femme.

Et s'il n'y avait plus de femmes.

Il serait où le début?

La Rivière Rouge est sinueuse. Elle a été façonné par l'eau. Elle est histoire. D'il y a des millénaires à aujourd'hui.

Et aujourd'hui, maintenant, nous sommes là pour l'écouter, les écouter.

Et vous?

Vous pouvez les entendre? Ces femmes, l'eau et leurs histoires. À vous de tendre l'oreille. C'est essentiel.

Tara Beagan has, with this world premiere, given voice to the past, present, and future.

Inspired by the work of the community organization Drag the Red, and working from the invitation to think about the climate crisis, this work gives voice to those whose voices have been taken here on Treaty 1 Territory.

It also gives a kind of hope.

Hope that family and community can hold us and that together we can move forward.

Hope that the power of story and community in our theatre spaces can effect change.

Hope and belief that we can, together, see our world for what it is and what it can be.

All of this, through an Indigenous-led project and process.

This project began on a foundation of trust between Tara, Prairie Theatre Exchange, and Théâtre Cercle Molière.

Four years since our first conversation, we first staged this play.

Three companies across two provinces. Three languages given breath.

One world premiere production that shook our hearts, minds, and spirits.

We are so grateful and proud to have brought about this production.

Thank you for being witness.

And for being a part of the story.

Geneviève Pelletier est une comédienne et metteuse en scène Métisse francophone de la Vallée de la Rivière Rouge. Depuis 2012, elle est directrice artistique du Théâtre Cercle Molière à Saint-Boniface. Elle s'intéresse à cultiver un espace créatif fertile qui accueille autant de cultures que de voix, qui reflète les diverses communautés avec lesquelles elle s'engage.

For over twenty-five years, Thomas Morgan Jones's work as a director, playwright, movement coach, dramaturg, and instructor has been seen nationally and internationally. He is currently Executive Artistic Director of the National Theatre School of Canada's English Section in Tiohtiáke, Montréal.

Rise, Red River was first produced by ARTICLE 11, Théâtre Cercle Molière, and Prairie Theatre Exchange in Treaty 1 Territory at Théâtre Cercle Molière, Winnipeg, from March 8 to 23, 2024, with the following cast and creative team:

She/Trip: Tracey Nepinak
Ancestor: Marsha Knight
All Other Women: Caleigh Crow

Director: Tara Beagan
Set, Lighting, and Video Design: Andy Moro
Costume Design: Tara Beagan and Andy Moro
Musical Composition and Sound Design: MJ Dandeneau
Choreographic Consultant: Christine Friday
Script Carrier: Charlene Van Buekenhout
French Translation: Natasha Kanapé Fontaine
Anishinaabemowin Translator and Coach: Wanda Barker
Métis Elder: Dolorès Gosselin
Stage Manager: Michelle Lagassé
Assistant Stage Manager: Bear Harper
Associate Artists: Thomas Morgan Jones and Geneviève Pelletier
Production Manager: Wayne Buss
Technical Director: Miguel Fortier
Assistant Technical Director: Patrick Bellemare
Props Master: Elana Honcharuk
Head of Wardrobe: Brenda McLean
Cutter/Stitcher: Claire Sparling
Stitchers: Heather Lee Brereton and Kate George
Carpenters: Keith Damboise and Steve Vande Vyvere
Scenic Artist and Sculptor: Melissa Smigelski
Foyer Art Installation: Jaime Black-Morsette
Technicians: Jenna Brown, Tommy Inthirath, Daniel Ross, and Cari Simpson
Surtitle Operator and Programmer: Jack Maier
Show Art: Jazz Aline

PLAYWRIGHT'S NOTES

The impetus for writing this play came from Thomas Morgan Jones, who suggested a play exploring climate change. With his prompt, and given his position as an artistic director in downtown Winnipeg, I immediately thought of Drag the Red and the incredible work they do. This work is dedicated to every woman who perseveres in spite of sorrow.

Funding for the playwright residency at Prairie Theatre Exchange (during the global pandemic and therefore out of residence) was entirely from the Canada Council for the Arts.

The workshop-ready draft came to fruition at the Banff Playwrights Lab in April 2022. The first artists to read the work aloud were Marie Beath Badian, Vickie Ramirez, and Monice Peter. I owe a debt of gratitude to all of the artists at the lab in '22 for their openness and courageous sharing, and to Brian Quirt, Jenna Rodgers, and Kodie Rollan for creating such a remarkable environment.

Throughout this process, dramaturgical supports have been Thomas Morgan Jones and Andy Moro.

CHARACTERS

She
This actor speaks English.

Ancestor
Grannie and/or Auntie Mags.
This actor speaks Anishinaabemowin.

The Women
"Woman," Lisa, Tanya, Rhonda.
This actor speaks French.

The three languages cross barriers and each woman comprehends one another.

1. FRACTURE / GAA-BOOKISEG / FRACTURE

Darkness and sound.

Many voices in English, French, and Anishinaabemowin:

Michi-babagidinaamon. Bigo gegoo izhiseg michi-bapagidinaamon.
Wiigonaamon.
Bagidinaamon.
Mii-gwayak.
Wiigonaamon.
Bagidinaamon.
Mii-iinzhi.

Ga'an gaye giga-biibaagisiimin. Ga'an awiya ji-gendang.
Amii gichi-wiikonaamon nindikwezensim. Haawn daga sa.

Just keep breathing. No matter what happens, just breathe.
In.
Out.
Good.
In.
Out.
That's it.
And we won't scream. No one can know.
Big breath in please now, my girl. C'mon!

Prends juste un grand respire.
Quoi qu'il arrive, prends juste une grande respiration.
Respire. Inspire. Expire. Quoi qu'il arrive, juste . . . respire.
Très bien.
Inspire.
Expire
Voilà, comme ça. C'est bon.
Nous n'allons pas crier. Personne doit savoir.
Prends un bonne inspiration, je t'en prie. Allez !

The sound of someone pushing through labour pain becomes the violent sounds of the earth cracking open.
The ground thunders louder than life.
After everything underground has been shaken out of place, quiet descends.
There is a buzzing and moaning in the quiet. We can hardly hear it.

Then, there is a woman.

We hear her before we see her.

SHE: Anne Marie, Rosslyn, Gertie, Jamie . . .

SHE *walks in a murky creek, one far smaller than its riverbed—hardly a dribble.* SHE *is weighted down by a large bundle on her back. It has all her essentials: a tin cup dangling from a loop; rolled-up tarps; some small bolts of cotton broadcloth in red, yellow, and black; and more. She has a smaller bundle bound securely to her front, which she soothes habitually, as though it is a sore stomach. Her clothes are made of scraps of leather and canvas, covered with brambles and dirt. Trailing behind her, attached to her by straps that encircle her shoulders and waist,*

SHE pulls a sort of improvised plough—three hooks welded together in a row.

It is evident SHE has been walking for some time.

Kaitlyn, Nancy, Lola, Danielle, Farrah, Esther, Samantha.

Please. Please. Please, someone . . .

Cassidy, Bertha, Nancy—
Wait. We already said Nancy. Though there must be more than one.

Hell.

SHE releases the plough and digs into her supplies.
SHE finds her precious water.
SHE pours some into her cup.
SHE sips it ever so lightly.
SHE pours a small amount into the cup again and bends down to the earth.

We seek, we gather, we collect. Water makes for walking.
Stories are for talking. Offering.

SHE pours the tiny amount of water onto the earth. A prayer. Unseen by SHE, but present on many levels, is an ANCESTOR presence. We see her shimmering in various frequencies, then disappearing. Her voice, though, is clear.

If anyone is listening. If anyone can help. Please.

ANCESTOR: Bapagidinaamon.
[Breathe.]

SHE: Keep walking.

SHE puts away the water and dons the hooks again.

ANCESTOR: Nishiime.
[My little sister.]

SHE: Ramona.

SHE closes her eyes and breathes.

Ramona was a crow. Smart. Cheeky. Ingenious. Always able to figure her way out of a tight spot. Until she couldn't. One day—one particularly sunny day when her nest and heart was full, a much bigger, meaner crow descended on the party, blocking everyone in. No. Scattering the chicks to the winds and trapping only Ramona. No. Hell.

SHE abruptly stops walking and talking, hardly noticing the plough has caught on something.

Hell.

ANCESTOR: Gwayak gida'ayaa.
[You're okay.]

SHE drops her plough and her bags. SHE digs through a bag that looks special. SHE pulls out a big antique tin can with a lid—a Blue Ribbon lard or Rogers Golden Syrup can, something iconic. SHE pops the lid, which is secured to the tin with a small chain. SHE pulls out a large set of rolled-up papers.

SHE: Ramona. Ramona, Ramona, Ramona . . . was a cashier at the grocery store . . . ah!

SHE finds the relevant notes and rereads them, facts only.

"High-risk lifestyle. Multiple reports of domestic abuse. Known to law enforcement"—ya, ya. Aaaaaand . . .

"Ramona's sister-in-law Denise, wife to Ramona's brother, reported that Ramona's brother appeared at her niece's birthday party, intoxicated and disruptive—" okay! We know this.

ANCESTOR: Gigikendaamin. Gibimiiwidoomin niibiwa awiya odibaajimowinan.
[We do. We carry the stories of so many.]

> SHE *rolls the documents back up, replaces them in the tin, puts the lid on, places the tin in the backpack.*
> SHE *picks up her load again and keeps ploughing, slower now.*

SHE: One day—one particularly sunny day, when her nest and heart was full, a much bigger, meaner crow descended on the party, scattering the chicks to the winds, and leaving only Ramona to fight for her life.

> SHE *continues pulling, all the while talking, when the plough unearths something/someone. It takes* SHE *a moment to notice.*

> ANCESTOR *appears in person, stands close to what is being dislodged.*

Ramona had grown up with nine siblings, all of whom were raised by their eldest sister, Margaret, after the passing of their mother when Ramona was only three years young.

> ANCESTOR *physically moves* SHE *so that* SHE *can see that she is hauling weight stuck on the plough.*

ANCESTOR: Bizindan gimiikinaawin!
[Listen to your trail!]

SHE: Holy smokes, it worked. Ramona?

2. FIRES / ISHKODEWINAN / INCENDIES

The thing catching the plough grows more dislodged. It is a woman. SHE *pulls until* WOMAN *fully emerges. The woman gasps, sitting upright, beating mud from her clothing.*

WOMAN: *(elle halète)* Je suis là! Je suis là!
[(gasps) I'm in here! I'm in here!]

The WOMAN *coughs and sputters, catches her breath.*

ANCESTOR: *(recognizing the woman)* Oshay!
[Oh, my.]

SHE: Ramona. Denise? Margaret?

WOMAN: Ohmaïgod ! J'peux pas respirer !
[Omigawd! I can't breathe!]

ANCESTOR *holds* WOMAN, *consoling her.* WOMAN *feels held, but nobody sees* ANCESTOR.

ANCESTOR: Mitagamig.
[Ground.]

SHE: You were in there a long time.

WOMAN: Je retenais mon souffle.
[I was holding my breath.]

SHE nods.

ANCESTOR: Babagidinaamon.
[Breathe.]

WOMAN: Nage pas. Où est . . . où est l'eau ?
[Don't swim. Where's the . . . the water?]

SHE: We know what you mean—holding your breath.

WOMAN suddenly moves away to get some distance from SHE, nearly frantic. ANCESTOR follows her, gently.

WOMAN: Oh my god . . . What the hell! Qu'est-ce qui s'est passé ?
[What happened?]

ANCESTOR breathes deeply and audibly, encouraging others to do the same.

SHE: Are you Ramona?

WOMAN: Je sais p . . . non. Je ne pense pas.
[I don't . . . no. I don't think so.]

SHE: That's okay. We just thought . . . we said her name. Or. No. We said lots of names, but then we said "Ramona" lots, and started to tell her story, and you know how stories are. Or Denise? Margaret?

"Margaret" twigs, but doesn't yet land.

WOMAN: Pas moi.
[Not me.]

SHE: Sorry. Um. Stick with what we know. You were underground. How did you get underground?

WOMAN: J'peux pas avoir choisi ça.
[It can't have been my choice.]

SHE: Likely not.

WOMAN: Holy shit. Comment on va faire pour le savoir ?
[How do we figure that out?]

SHE: "Holy shit."

ANCESTOR: Gigikendaan giin iwe gidibaajimowin.
[You know your own story.]

The WOMAN hears ANCESTOR's voice as her own thoughts.

SHE: What's the last thing you remember?

ANCESTOR: Awenen gidinawemaaganag?
[Who's your family?]

The WOMAN breathes and thinks. SHE is patient.

WOMAN: Comment est-ce qu'on . . . ? N'importe quoi ?
[How do we . . . ? Anything?]

SHE: Anything is easy. Anything is anything that isn't nothing. What we need is to get you to remember that you're not nothing.

WOMAN: Et ça, c'est où ?
[Where is this?]

SHE: We're in the Red River.

WOMAN: Comment . . . ?
[How . . . ?]

The WOMAN *finds soil on herself and considers its texture, colour—is it like the earth at home?*

ANCESTOR: Gigikendaamin miziwe owe aki aaniish inaa biinja'ii gigii-miinigowisimin.
[The map of the land is in our blood.]

SHE: We're just a couple hours' walk from the dam.

WOMAN: Ouais, je . . . on vient de plus loin au nord d'ici. Ça s'fait pas à pied. Trop loin . . . J'ai étudié sur les gens arrachés à leur famille. C'était pour ma thèse. J'ai tellement essayé de visiter chaque communauté. De voir les territoires. Les peuples. De rencontrer leur deuil. Leurs rivières.
[Yeah, I . . . we're from way north of here. Further than a walk. So far . . . I studied stolen people. As part of my Ph.D. work. Tried hard to visit each community. To see the land. People. Meet their grief. Their rivers.]

SHE: Sounds good.

WOMAN: Les enfants comme Harmony . . . y se font envoyer ailleurs pour l'école secondaire. Les communautés d'où ils viennent ont pas d'écoles secondaires, right ? Et la plupart des enfants ont jamais été à l'extérieur avant. Y'ont le vertige juste à regarder des immeubles d'appartements.
[Kids like Harmony . . . they get sent away for high school. Their home communities don't have high schools, right? And some of these kids had never been away before. Get vertigo just from looking up at apartment buildings.]

ANCESTOR: Geniin sago.
[Same as me.]

WOMAN: Comme Grannie Mags. Ha ! Grannie Mags.
[Like my Grannie Mags. Huh! Grannie Mags.]

SHE: Her name?

ANCESTOR: *(touching ground)* Gibimiiwinigoo.
[We carry you.]

WOMAN: Elle m'a élevée. Mon arrière-grand-tante, en vrai. Mais je l'appelais Grannie Mags.
[She raised me. My great-great-aunt, actually. But I called her Grannie Mags.]

SHE: That's a good start.

WOMAN: Oui. C'était.
[It was.]

SHE: "Vertigo."

WOMAN: C'est quand tu es un peu étourdi. Ou déstabilisé. T'as l'impression que le monde pourrait chavirer.
[It's when you get kind of dizzy. Or thrown off balance. Feels like the world might tip over.]

SHE: We've had that. But when our eyes are closed.

WOMAN: Est-ce que vous, vous tombez ?
[Do youse fall?]

SHE: Sometimes.

SHE feels the ground with her hands.

SHE: Did she?

WOMAN: Ma Grannie Mags ?
[My Grannie Mags?]

SHE: Yes.

WOMAN: Presque. Mais c'est là qu'elle s'est souvenue qu'elle a des racines.
[Almost. But then she remembered she has roots.]

ANCESTOR: Nimashkikii'ikwe ikwezens.
[My doctor girl.]

Beat.

SHE: And the kids?

WOMAN: Ils se perdent. Leurs racines sont avec eux, mais ils pouvaient juste pas les ressentir. Trop loin de la maison.
[They get lost. Their roots are with them, but they just couldn't seem to feel them. So far from home.]

ANCESTOR: Odibaajimowiniyaa.
[Their stories.]

Beat.

WOMAN: Harmony. Le système lui avait collé la mention de suicide et a fermé son dossier. C'est pourquoi je suis devenue intervenante sociale chez nous.
[Harmony. The system branded her a suicide and filed her away. It's why I became a social worker.]

SHE: "Became."

WOMAN: Harmony. Une jeune femme—une jeune fille, vraiment—à peine treize ans. Elle était l'aînée de sept—toutes des sœurs.
[Harmony. A young woman—a girl, really—only thirteen. She was the eldest of seven—all sisters.]

ANCESTOR: Dookinan aki.
[Touch ground.]

WOMAN connects to the earth.

WOMAN: Son récit ressemblait beaucoup à celui de ma Grannie Mags. Sa mère est morte quand elle était toute petite, aussi. Donc elle et ses sœurs ont été toutes placées. Certaines ensemble, la plupart non.
[Her story sounded a lot like my Grannie Mags's. Her mom died when she was pretty small, too. So her and all her sisters got fostered out. Some together, mostly not.]

Elle était la première à aller à l'école secondaire dans le sud.
[She was the first to go south for high school.]

Pauvre 'tite. Elle avait été montée d'un niveau parce qu'elle était tellement intelligente. Après qu'elle soit décédée, on a trouvé ses écrits dans un ordinateur de l'école. Elle n'en avait pas un, mais elle passait son temps à la bibliothèque.
[Poor thing. She had been put ahead a grade because of how bright she was. After she died, they found some writing from her on a school computer. She didn't have her own, but she was at the library all hours.]

On a trouvé ses mots là-dedans :
« C'est trop dur d'être une fille autochtone. »
« C'est trop dur d'être une fille autochtone. »
[They found her words there:
"It's too hard to be an Indigenous girl."
"It's too hard to be an Indigenous girl."]

Partout, partout, partout sur l'écran. Des pages de ça. Cette grande petite fille s'assoyait là, effrayée et toute seule, trop loin de la maison, en sachant que ses sœurs passeraient éventuellement toutes par le même enfer. Pis elle ne pouvait pas porter ça.
[Over and over and over on the screen. Pages of it. That big little girl sat there, afraid and alone, too far from home, knowing all of her

sisters would eventually be put through the same hell. And she couldn't carry that.]

ANCESTOR: Ogii-bwaanetoon ji-bimiiwidood iwe, dago wiin. Zhigo Tessa . . .
[Couldn't carry that as well as herself. And Tessa . . .]

WOMAN: Ma nièce, Tessa—
[My niece, Tessa—]

SHE: Tessa.

WOMAN: —elle a quinze ans. Tellement brillante. Elle organisait ma recherche pour moi. Elle s'est investie à fond dans leurs histoires. Ces enfants en mal de chez eux. Mais spécialement dans l'histoire d'Harmony.
[—she's fifteen. So smart. She was logging my research for me. She got so invested in their stories. Those homesick kids. But especially Harmony's.]

ANCESTOR: Ninzaagii-aayens Lisa.
[My sweet Lisa.]

WOMAN: Un jour elle m'a dit, « Matante Lisa »—
[One day she said to me, "Auntie Lisa—"]

LISA's voice stops abruptly.

SHE: Lisa!

LISA: Lisa. Oui. Matante Lisa. Tessa. Grannie Mags.
[Lisa. Yes. Auntie Lisa. Tessa. Grannie Mags.]

Beat.

Il fallait qu'on parte. Ils nous ont déplacés. À cause des feux.
[We had to leave. They moved us. Because of the fires.]

SHE: That happened a lot.

LISA: On était supposé de revenir après.
[Supposed to go back after.]

SHE: Our story is a lot like yours.

LISA: L'histoire de qui ?
[Whose?]

SHE: *(direct echo of how LISA said it)* "Whose?"

LISA: Tu fais ça souvent.
[You do that a lot.]

SHE: Do what a lot?

LISA: Répéter ce que je dis.
[Repeat what I say.]

SHE: We spent a long time listening. It's how we learn.

LISA nods.

LISA: Et c'est qui ton « nous »?
[And who's your "we"?]

SHE: Can you repeat that?

LISA: Tu dis toujours « nous ». Et « notre ». Mais je vois personne d'autre. Donc . . . tu parles de qui quand tu dis « nous »?
[You always say "we." And "our." But I don't see anyone else. So . . . who do you mean when you say "we"?]

SHE: Oh. Us, *(SHE and LISA)* I guess.

LISA: Mais j'viens de te rencontrer.
[But I just met you.]

SHE: Maybe not.

LISA nods, but with some confusion.

There is more inquiring she'd like to do, but she holds back, uncertain of where she stands.

The herds were driven south by the fires, too.

LISA: Redis ça encore ?
[Say again?]

SHE: You were saying "We had to leave. They moved us. Because of the fires. Supposed to go back after."

LISA: Oui, on . . . on devait s'en retourner après. Moi, Tessa, et Grannie Mags.
[Yeah, we . . . we were. Me, Tessa, and Grannie Mags.]

SHE: "We were."

LISA: Ou. Pour vrai, ils étaient supposés nous ramener après.
[Or. Really, they were supposed to take us back after.]

SHE: After the fires.

LISA: Ouais.
[Ya.]

SHE: But then the hurricanes came.

LISA: Je . . . je suis pas sûre de ça.
[I don't . . . think so.]

SHE: Oh.

LISA: J'suis pas sûre que les feux ont fini par arrêter.
[I don't think the fires ever stopped.]

SHE: They did. Just took a few years.

LISA: Holy shit.

SHE: Once they spread to the tar sands, it . . . everything burned.

LISA: Jesus.

SHE: Bones started surfacing. Heated earth, cracking concrete. All the bones began to show.

LISA: On peut les ressentir.
[You can feel them.]

SHE: And then the rain. Flooding. Hurricanes.

LISA: Comment je suis arrivée ici ?
[How did I get here?]

Beat.

SHE: We can try to find out. Here, we have this thing. It's what got us looking so far in the first place. It even says "Lisa" on it in a few places.

SHE pulls out her tin can of documents.

LISA: No way.

LISA reaches out to hold the can, so SHE surrenders it.

Est-ce que c'est à ma grannie ? Non. Beaucoup de monde ont une canne comme ça aussi, non ?
[Is this my grannie's? No. Lots of people have this tin, right?]

SHE: Just you, for now.

ANCESTOR: Giinawind owe. Gakina giinawind.
[It's ours. All of us.]

LISA opens it. She sees the chain someone added to tether the lid, recognizes it.

SHE: It was in the dirt at the Forks. We looked at it—no.

She practises using "I" very deliberately.

I looked at it a long time. And then the shapes became sounds, and I could learn from them, too.

ANCESTOR: Gigii-anamitamoon.
[I read it to you.]

SHE: Started reading it. Learning. Then longing.

LISA pulls the rolls of documents out.

LISA: C'est ma thèse de doctorat. Sur nos femmes disparues. Et nos filles. Et nos personnes two-spirit. J'veux dire, jesus ! Pas toutes d'entre elles. Je me suis penchée sur des cas interconnectés. Il y avait tellement de cicatrices, comme des ficelles, dans chaque famille. Même dans la nôtre.
[This is my Ph.D. research. Into our stolen women. And girls. And two-spirits. I mean, jesus! Not all of them. I was looking into interconnected cases. There were so many scars threaded through families. Even ours.]

ANCESTOR: Ningii-ningwa'aan.
[I buried it.]

SHE: Someone buried it by the rivers.

ANCESTOR: Ji gananjigaaded.
[Safekeeping.]

LISA sits and sets the can and the documents down, so overwhelmed.
She breathes.
She looks into the can again and finds a small hand-rolled cigarette inside, holding it up.

LISA: Grannie Mags.

She inhales the smell of the tobacco.

Elle l'a probablement enterré où . . . Sûrement qu'elle me pleure là-bas. Qu'est-ce-qui est arrive ?! What the hell?!
[She probably buried it where . . . She probably mourns me there. What the hell happened?]

SHE: *(quietly)* "Hell."

Beat.

We can make another map.

LISA: Nous sommes la mappe.
[We are the map.]

ANCESTOR: Gidibaajimowininaan.
[Our story.]

SHE: Good maps start with who we are and where. You're sure your name is Lisa?

ANCESTOR: Eya.
[Yes.]

LISA: Mon nom est Lisa.
[My name is Lisa.]

SHE sets the research onto the soil.

SHE: There's you. And you have a niece named Tessa.

LISA: Oui. Je suis Matante Lisa.
[Yes. I'm Auntie Lisa.]

SHE takes a few pages of the research and folds it down smaller, to symbolize Tessa, and sets it beside LISA.

SHE: That's good.

ANCESTOR: Lisa. Tessa. Margaret.

SHE: And your great-aunt Grannie?

LISA: Elle était le feu de la maison.
[She was the homefire.]

LISA sets her hands firmly on the soil.
Then she picks up the tin and sets it down to symbolize Margaret.

Grannie Mags. Mon arrière-grand-tante Margaret. Sa petite sœur, la grand-mère de ma mère, s'appelait Ohna. Elle est morte bien avant ma naissance. Mais j'ai entendu des histoires par contre. Elle était tough.
[Grannie Mags. My great-great-auntie Margaret. Her little sister, my mom's grandma, she was called Ohna. She passed long before I was born. I heard stories, though. She was tough.]

SHE detaches the lid from the tin and sets it in its own space, as a symbol for Ohna.

SHE: And your mom?

LISA's hands are fully nested in the soil now.

LISA: Je ne . . . Je ne l'ai jamais connue.
[I don't . . . I didn't ever know her.]

ANCESTOR: Niminjinawez.
[I'm so sorry.]

LISA: Ma Grannie Mags l'a élevée, elle aussi. Mais elle a disparu. Grannie avait de la misère à parler d'elle. Nous ne savons pas ce qui s'est passé.
[My Grannie Mags raised her, too. But she disappeared. Gran had a hard time talking about her. We don't know what happened.]

LISA makes clear handprints in the soil as a symbol for LISA's mom, separate from the others.

Elle est sortie un soir. Elle a été séparée de ses amies. Il y a eu des rumeurs selon lesquelles elle aurait été vue à l'arrière d'une voiture de police, mais . . . / On le sait pas.
[She went out one night. Got separated from friends. There were rumours she was seen in the back of a cop car, but . . . / we don't know.]

ANCESTOR: Gaawiin ningikendasiimin.
[We don't know.]

SHE: So sorry.

LISA: Disparue.
[Disappeared.]

SHE: Lisa, do you know if you disappeared?

LISA: Je sais pas comment . . . le savoir.
[I don't know how to . . . know that.]

SHE: It's just . . . there are a few Lisas who got stolen. Or went missing. Or . . .

LISA: Tu le sais grâce à mes recherches.
[You know this from my research.]

SHE: *(pointing at the documents)* These.

LISA: Mais mes dossiers peuvent pas nous dire ce qui m'est arrivé.
[But my files can't tell us what happened to me.]

ANCESTOR: Gaawiin memech ji-gendaman.
[You don't need to know.]

SHE: But maybe now—now that you're here, with me—maybe they can.

> *LISA brushes the soil off her hands as if she was rubbing precious oils into them.*

LISA: J'ai besoin de savoir.
[I need to know.]

> *ANCESTOR nods and dances some calm in preparation for the map-making.*

SHE: Um. Okay. People. Lisa. Tessa. Margaret. Ohna.

> *A beat when they all acknowledge LISA's missing mom.*

Simultaneously:

ANCESTOR: Rhonda.

LISA: Rhonda.

SHE: Rhonda. And what about places?

LISA: Le Nord. La Fourche. La Ville. Le barrage de Lockport ?
[The North. The Forks. The City. Lockport dam?]

SHE nods as she draws the map.

Si Lockport est ici, ma communauté est plus haut ici.
[If Lockport is here, our community is up here.]

LISA moves the symbols for herself, placing Tessa and Grannie Mags up north. The symbol for Rhonda—the handprints—becomes the City.

SHE: How far each way does the land go?

LISA: Vers les océans. Je suppose que c'est à peu près ici. Et ici. Et là.
[To the oceans. I guess about to here. And here. And there.]

LISA and SHE draw Turtle Island's full coastline.

SHE: And the river comes from the south.

SHE extends the Red River path.

It's a good start. Maybe now . . . what's the first thing you remember clearly?

LISA: La première première ? Jesus . . .
[Ever? Jesus . . .]

SHE: I meant . . . what's the most recent thing you remember clearly?

ANCESTOR clarifies and grounds LISA's memory through movement and song.
During this, LISA adds story to the soil map.

LISA: On avait un meeting à 2h. Avec le Downtown Business Association. Et quelques propriétaires d'hôtels. Les incendies ont été . . . Les incendies ont duré combien de temps ?
[We had a meeting at two. With the Downtown Business Association. And some hotel owners. The fires were . . . How long did the fires last?]

SHE: The last ones went on for about three years.

LISA: Trois ANS ?
[Three YEARS?]

As LISA learns of the destruction in the world, ANCESTOR's movements absorb the impact as well, to help LISA be present as long as she wishes to.

SHE: After a few months people couldn't see each other across the street. After three years, mostly they weren't there anymore.

LISA: Regardez ce que nous avons fait.
[Look what we've done.]

ANCESTOR: Oganawenjigeg ogii-doodaanaawaa' ayiiminik gaa-ishkitoowaad.
[The protectors did what they could.]

LISA: Les Gardiens de la Terre ne pouvaient pas porter tout ça. En plus d'eux—mêmes.
[The protectors couldn't carry all that. As well as themselves.]

SHE: The money people did not believe the fires would spread all over.

LISA: Ils ne s'attendent jamais au pire. Nous, on le fait toujours. C'est l'un des rares avantages d'avoir un trauma ancestral.
[They never expect the worst. We always do. It's one of the few perks of ancestral trauma.]

SHE bursts out laughing.

ANCESTOR: *(relieved to see their humour/strength)* Na imaa giinawind.
[There we are.]

LISA: J'imagine que c'est assez drole.
[I guess that is kinda funny.]

SHE: Sad funny.

LISA: Il reste qui ? J'veux dire—désolée. J'ai tout fait ça à l'envers. Aaniin. J'suis Lisa. Enchantée.
[Who's left? I mean—sorry. I've done this all backwards. Aaniin. I'm Lisa. It's nice to meet you.]

SHE: Aaniin? Is Aaniin me?

LISA: Oh, je . . . je connais pas ton nom. Je disais juste salut.
[Oh. I . . . I don't know your name. I was just saying hi.]

SHE: Oh.

LISA: Désolée.
[Sorry.]

SHE: It's not your fault. Sometimes hope comes outta nowhere.

Beat.

It's nice to meet you, Lisa, Tessa's auntie. Margaret and Rhonda and Ohna's girl.

LISA: Ma mère a été envoyée chez ma Grannie Mags. Après que sa mère soit morte.
[My mom was sent to Grannie Mags. After her mom died.]

SHE: So many moms missing.

ANCESTOR: Nishiime. Odaanisan. Gimaamaa.
[My sister. Her daughter. Your mom.]

LISA: Qui est ta famille ? Ton peuples ?
[Who is your family? Your people?]

SHE: You're the first person I've found. I've been alone.

ANCESTOR: Gaawiin wiikaa gibezhigosii.
[Never alone.]

LISA: Nous ne sommes jamais seules.
[We're never alone.]

SHE: So. You. You're my people.

LISA: Mais je pense pas te connaître.
[But I don't think I know you.]

SHE: Oh.

LISA: Mais on se connait maintenant !
[But we do now!]

ANCESTOR: Inawemaaganag.
[Family.]

SHE: Yes. Um . . . Do you know any times?

LISA: C'était en juillet. Quand nous avons quitté la maison. On allait manquer le retour des saskatoons. Ils ont entassé six ou huit personnes dans une chambre de motel. Mais c'était tellement un soulagement de pouvoir avoir de l'eau. On en mettait de côté quand on pouvait. Parce qu'on le savait que ça pouvait arrêter de couler du robinet n'importe quand.
[It was July. When we left home. We were gonna miss seeing if the berries came back. They stuffed six or eight people in a motel room. But it was so nice to have water again. We were saving it in everything we could get hold of. Because we knew it could run out.]

SHE: It has.

LISA: Certains d'entre nous, membres du conseil, on rencontrait les propriétaires d'hôtels et les représentants de la ville.
[Some of us on council were meeting with the hotels and the city reps.]

SHE: At two.

LISA: Jesus christ quelle perte de temps.
[Jesus christ, what a waste of time.]

SHE: Our people were sheltered in school gyms, arenas, industrial warehouses . . .

LISA: Toutes ces chambres fancy vides ! Et des reconnaissances territoriales dans chaque lobby. Fucking assholes. Je parie qu'ils ont fini par placer de ces . . . « allies » . . . dans chaque endroit.
[All those fancy empty rooms! And land acknowledgements in every lobby. Fucking assholes. Bet they ended up putting up . . . "allies" . . . in those places.]

SHE: White people.

LISA: Ouais. Comment tu fais pour continuer ?
[Yeah. How do you keep going?]

SHE: How did you?

ANCESTOR: Ningii-wiiji'igoo.
[With help.]

LISA: Ouais. J'ai eu de l'aide. Jamais de la part de mes supposés collègues, mais de ma famille. Toujours. Même le conseil de bande de merde a refusé ma demande de financement pour mon doctorat. Des bullies de merde j'te dis.
[Yeah. I had help. Never from my so-called colleagues, but family. Always. The damn band even declined my application for funding for my doctorate. Damn bullies.]

SHE: So, how did you gather so many stories?

LISA: Grannie Mags. Elle travaillait depuis l'âge de douze ans. Elle économisait. Cash. Dans cette boîte de conserve. Elle avait 92 ans quand elle me l'a donnée. La canne était pleine à ras bord ! Elle a dit qu'elle savait que ça allait venir. Qu'un jour ça servirait. J'allais la repayer pour ça. Même si elle voulait pas que je le fasse.
[Grannie Mags. She'd been working since she was twelve. Saving up. Cash. In that tin can. She was ninety-two when she handed it to me. That thing was stuffed! Said she knew there'd be a reason for it eventually. I was gonna pay her back. Even though she said not to.]

ANCESTOR: Gizaagii'in.
[I love you.]

LISA remembers the rollie in the tin can.

SHE: Do you want something to eat? Or drink?

LISA: Merci. Peut-être qu'on peut faire une offrande ?
[Thank you. Maybe we can make an offering?]

SHE: Okay.

SHE passes LISA the food bundle. LISA takes some food and holds it in her left hand, against her heart, like tobacco. SHE follows her lead, learning this for the first time.

LISA and SHE place some food into the soil. LISA then breaks the rollie open and puts half of it into the earth, keeping the rest.

ANCESTOR: Miigwech.

ANCESTOR prays silently.

LISA: Si j'étais retournée chez moi, j'aurais trouvé quoi ?
[If I went home, what would there be?]

SHE: Everything in the north was ashes. And maybe fireweed by now. Some grasses? Maybe?

LISA: Je serais retournée vers rien. Encore. Les prédateurs rôdent vraiment quand ça arrive. Encore et encore. Nos jeunes se font jeter dans un monde avec des étrangers, et ils se font prendre pour être emmenés ailleurs.
[No home to go back to. Again. The predators really circle when that happens. Over and over. Our young ones are shunted out into a world of strangers, and they get taken.]

SHE: Young ones are so bright. So quiet.

ANCESTORS: Anangoog.
[Stars.]

ANCESTOR shimmers stars across the sky.
SHE touches ground.
LISA takes in SHE's getup and the plough.

LISA: Quand est-ce que t'as commencé à traîner cette chose partout ?
[When did you start dragging this thing around?]

SHE: I learned about the hooks in your research. I read about them and the boat that used to pull them through the water. The people who used to search for their missing people. Then I found the hooks! It all lined up to make a path. So I walked it.

LISA: Tu fais rien à moitié, toi non ?
[You don't do anything halfway, do you?]

SHE: Not that I remember.

LISA: Depuis combien de temps que tu marches comme ça ?
[How long have you been walking?]

SHE looks all around her, at how impossible everything is.

SHE: I don't know how to know that.

ANCESTOR: Babagidinaamon. Bazangwaabin.
[Breathe. Close your eyes.]

LISA and SHE both close their eyes and breathe.

LISA: Le ciel bleu. Des baies mûres. Du pickerel frais. Les linges à vaisselle de Grannie, lavées à l'eau de javel et séchées au soleil.
[Blue skies. Ripe berries. Fresh pickerel. The bleach and sunshine clean of Grannie's tea towels.]

ANCESTOR: Giin gidayaa omaa ji-maamikawiyan.
[You remain to remember.]

LISA opens her eyes.

LISA: Il me reste rien. Comment se termine mon histoire ?
[All gone. How does my story end?]

LISA sits down on the ground.

SHE: What was it that Tessa asked?

LISA: De quoi ?
[What?]

SHE: When she was helping you with your work. You said she asked, "Auntie Lisa . . . ?"

LISA: « Matante Lisa, comment qu'une fille de treize ans pouvait savoir c'était quoi le suicide »?
["Auntie Lisa . . . how did a thirteen-year-old girl even know about suicide?"]

Beat.

Je savais tellement pas quoi lui répondre. Tout ce qui me venait à l'esprit, c'était Tessa elle-même, deux ans avant quand elle avait treize ans, qui sautait sur sa trampoline jusqu'à la lune, les lèvres teintées du bleu de ses bonbons.
[I had no idea what to tell her. All I could think of was Tessa two years ago, thirteen herself, and jumping high as the moon on her trampoline, lips tinted bright blue from junk food.]

SHE: Thirteen-year-old girls. We don't have those anymore either.

LISA: Je suis venue au bord de l'eau avant le meeting. Peut-être que j'ai sauté.
[I came to the water before the meeting. Maybe I jumped.]

SHE: Into the river?

LISA: Mais je n'aurais pas fait ça. Pour moi je sais que les rivières sont faites pour donner la vie.
[But I wouldn't have. I understand the rivers are meant to give life.]

SHE: When the fires had been going for a while all the water warmed up. Lakes, creeks, even this river.

LISA: Ce serait vraiment grave.
[That would be bad.]

SHE: Just like the heated soil, they're forced to give up their secrets. Things they've hidden. People they've killed.

LISA: Les rivières tuent rarement des gens. Les gens tuent les gens. Ça te fait réaliser à quel point les morts nous dépassent de leur nombre.
[Rivers rarely kill people. People kill people. Makes you realize how outnumbered we are. By the dead.]

SHE: Yeah.

Beat.

LISA: Les blancs.
[White people.]

SHE: Yeah, them too.

LISA: Non, ils . . . J'étais au bord de la rivière. Je déposais une offrande. Et des blancs ont commencé à m'interpeller.
[No, they . . . I was at the river. Making an offering. And some white guys started calling me out.]

SHE: What do you mean?

LISA: On m'avait appris à me présenter à l'eau, où qu'on aille. Faire une offrande. Écouter.
[Was taught to introduce myself to the water, wherever we went. Make an offering. Listen.]

SHE: Sounds good.

LISA: Avant le meeting. J'ai marché jusqu'à la rivière. Et les *assholes* ont commencé à me hurler après parce que pour eux je laissais des déchets. Ils ont demandé à voir mon permis de pêche.
[Before the meeting. I walked down to the river. And these assholes *start yelling at me for littering. Ask to see my fishing licence.]*

ANCESTOR: Daga gaawiin.
[(doesn't want it to be true) Please.]

LISA: Pis ils m'ont . . . non. J'veux pas ça.
[And they . . . no. I don't want this.]

> *LISA hugs SHE, as though hiding in her. SHE is nearly knocked over by how much she needed this hug.*

SHE: Oh!

LISA: J'veux pas que mon histoire se termine comme ça.
[I don't want my story to end like this.]

SHE: They asked to see your fishing licence. And then you asked to see their hunting licence.

LISA: Quoi ?
[What?]

> *LISA pulls out of the hug to look into SHE's face.*
> *Traces of deer appear.*

SHE: The river was running pretty normal—murky and swift. Lots of bank to stand on. Bit mucky here and there, but solid enough. You step carefully as they shout at you, ready to run. But you know they don't have a hunting licence. And so you make an offering to the water and it washes over you, revealing you to be a beautiful doe.

LISA: Plus rapide que n'importe quel homme blanc.
[Faster than any white man.]

SHE: They don't have a hunting licence and they don't have a hunting rifle and they don't have long lean legs and a cotton white tail to flick "goodbye" as they leap away. And you leap away. Running for miles. And you will never hear their voices again. Safe and safe and safe.

LISA hangs her clothing among the trees, like the now-famed Red Dresses, and then she vanishes into the herd, eventually standing with ANCESTOR, shimmering.

Deer leap and play all around, then run far away.

(like praying) We miss you.

Simultaneously:

ANCESTOR: Omaa nindayaamin.
[We're here.]

LISA: Nous sommes ici.
[We're here.]

SHE: This land is a map. Every day I learn better how to read.

SHE considers the people symbols and place markers.

Lisa. Lisa's great-great-aunt is Margaret: Grannie Mags. Lisa's great-grandma is Ramona. Ramona and Margaret are sisters. Lisa's mom, raised up by Grannie Mags is Rhonda. Rhonda disappeared. And Rhonda's mom?

ANCESTOR: Tanya.

LISA: La mère de Rhonda s'appelait Tanya.
[Rhonda's mom was called Tanya.]

SHE: Lisa's mom is Rhonda. Rhonda's mom is . . .

ANCESTOR: Tanya gimaamaa omaamaayan. Eya.
[Tanya was your mom's mom. Yes.]

LISA: Et Tanya, elle . . . ?
[And Tanya, she . . . ?]

ANCESTOR: Gewiin gii-odaapinaa.
[Was stolen, too.]

SHE: *(rather quietly)* Lisa? She was gonna be my people.

LISA: Je le suis.
[I am.]

ANCESTOR: Nindayaamin.
[We are.]

SHE: We are.

ANCESTOR: Gakina dibaajimowinan boonisewan.
[Every story ends.]

LISA: Et continue. Quand elle est racontée.
[And carries on. When carried.]

SHE: Lisa's mom is Rhonda.

LISA: Qui est sa *(en référence à* SHE*)* mère ? Et qui est-elle ?
[Who is her (referring to SHE*) mom? And who is she?]*

ANCESTOR and LISA put the hook plough back on SHE.

SHE: Lisa! Come back!

Beat.

Someone. Please!

ANCESTOR: Bebezhig eta'go gidakokiimin.
[One step at a time.]

ANCESTOR stands in front of SHE and guides her—they walk. LISA falls away, transitioning into another woman.

SHE: Anyone! Please!

ANCESTOR: Babagidinaamon.
[Breathe.]

SHE: Lisa is my people. Rhonda is Lisa's mom. Who can be my mom?

Panic lands.

SOMEONE!

SHE struggles to ground.

We seek, we gather, we collect, we bottle. Water makes for walking. Stories are for talking. Offering.

SHE starts running all over the map and people symbols. For the first time ANCESTOR is not alongside her.

Lisa! Tessa! Margaret! Ohna! Rhonda!
Lisa! Tessa! Margaret! Ohna! Rhonda!
Lisa! Tessa! Margaret! Ohna! Rhonda!
Harmony! Harmony! Harmony!

SHE keeps ploughing and slows to walking.

Dammit. Lisa! Lisa?

SHE pauses a moment, listens, then keeps ploughing, slowly, depleted.

Listen to the trail. Breathe. Walk. Never alone.

ANCESTOR reappears.

ANCESTOR: Omaa gidaayaamin.
[We're here.]

SHE closes her eyes and breathes.

SHE: Ramona was a woman. Smart. Cheeky. Ingenious. Always able to figure her way out of a tight spot. Until she couldn't. One day, one particularly sunny day when her nest and heart was full, a much bigger, meaner crow descended on the party, scattering the chicks to the winds, leaving only Ramona to fight for her life.

But there was someone. Just there. Hiding and hoping. A baby Ramona had had five years ago. A baby girl whose birthday cake had just been shared.

ANCESTOR: Omaa gidayaamin.
[We're here.]

SHE sets down her plough.
She recalls LISA's teachings.

SHE: "Introduce myself to the water." "Make an offering." "Listen."

SHE finds some good food in her bundle and creates a small feast offering.

She finishes with some tobacco.

Sisters, if you come to me, we will reveal your stories as you choose.

You deserve to have a telling. I call on you to help me, and I will help you, in turn.

Beat.

Sissy, Taylor, Alberta, Harmony, Wilma, Dorothy, Violet, Odette, Beverly, Marian . . . Lisa, Tessa, Margaret, Ohna, Rhonda. Who is Rhonda's mom?

WOMAN enters as TANYA. SHE doesn't yet see her. ANCESTOR does.

ANCESTOR: Tanya.

3. FAMINE / MANDAWIIWEWIN / FAMINE

SHE: We deserve to have a telling.

SHE resumes her ploughing. The plough catches on an old bust-ed-up fake-leather purse. SHE doesn't notice.

WOMAN and ANCESTOR agree on something unspoken. WOMAN crouches in the dirt and starts digging around, searching.

Listen to the trail. Breathe. Walk. Never alone.

SHE walks right by TANYA without seeing her.

Sisters, if you come to me, we will reveal your stories as you choose.

TANYA: Hey! Je cherche . . .
[I'm looking for . . .]

Coughs indelicately. Spits. Horks. Coughs some more.

S'cuse-moi. Oh, super. Maintenant j'ai sûrement une fucking TB ou quelque chose de même. Fuck.
['Scuse me. Oh, great. Now I probably have fucking TB or something.]

SHE: Aaniin.

TANYA: Pardonnez-vous ?
[Pardon you?]

SHE: Um. You look a lot like . . . are . . . are you related to Lisa?

ANCESTOR: Tanya.

TANYA: À qui ai-je l'honneur ?
[Who's asking?]

SHE: Oh, we're . . . *(correcting the "we")* I'm Aaniin.

TANYA: Hein ?
[Huh?]

SHE: Just kidding. I said . . . I'm an auntie.

TANYA: Oh. Je pensais que tu avais dit « sœur ».
[I thought you said "sister."]

SHE: Right. But you're so young. Feels more like maybe I could be your auntie.

TANYA: Les aunties peuvent être plus jeunes. Je connaissais une fille, une fois—elle, elle avait dix-sept ans, et sa auntie était en quatrième année.
[Aunties can be younger. I knew this girl, once—she was seventeen and she had an auntie in grade four.]

SHE: Wow.

TANYA: Elle avait cinquante-huit cousins.
[She had fifty-eight cousins.]

SHE: Okay.

TANYA: Cette fille, c'était moi.
[That person was me.]

SHE: Oh, wow. You have fifty-eight cousins?

TANYA: C'est la rumeur.
[That's the rumour.]

Beat.

Non. Je mens. Ou, non. J'en fais le souhait.
[No. I'm lying. Or, no. I'm wishing.]

SHE: Or you're praying.

TANYA: *(se souvient soudain)* Attends ! *(avec urgence)* Je cherche mon sac à main !
[(recalling with urgency) Hold up! I'm looking for my purse!]

SHE: Well . . . all right.

ANCESTOR: Tanya giwaabam na?
[Tanya, do you see me?]

TANYA sees the food and tobacco offering in the soil. She digs out the food and eats it.

TANYA: Donc tu l'es ou tu l'es pas ?
[So are you or aren't you?]

SHE: What?

TANYA: Ma auntie.
[My auntie.]

ANCESTOR: Niin gosha gimaamaayens.
[I'm your auntie.]

SHE: Eeeeeee-yes?

TANYA: Hm.

Beat.

SHE: You hungry?

TANYA: Dah ! Je viens de manger quelques chose que j'ai trouvé dans la boue là-bas. J'ai même pas partagé. Affamée la fille ! Et aussi, j'suis Tanya. Pas Marian. Pas Odette. Je connais pas de « Marian » ou « Odette ». Je connais une Margaret, mais je suis pas elle. Et j'ai connu quelqu'un qui s'appelait Ohna, mais son vrai nom c'était RA-mona.
[Duh! I just finished eating something I found in the dirt over there. I didn't even share. That's hungry! And I'm also Tanya. Not Marian. Or Odette. I dunno no "Marian." Or "Odette." I know a Margaret, but I'm not her. And I knew someone called Ohna, but her real name was RA-mona.]

SHE hands TANYA some dried meat. TANYA sits down to eat. ANCESTOR sits beside her, rapt.

ANCESTOR: Gesa ginwenzh.
[It's been so long.]

SHE: Did you say you know Margaret and Ohna?

TANYA: RA-mona. Laisse tomber.
[RA-mona. Drop it.]

ANCESTOR: Nishiime.
[My sister.]

TANYA: Malade ! Est-ce que c'est de l'orignal ?
[Wild! Is this moose?]

SHE: Yes?

TANYA: J'en ai pas eu depuis que j'étais petite.
[Haven't had this since I was a kid.]

ANCESTOR: Ningii-wiindamaagoomin egii-niboyan enitaawigi'ad Rhonda. *[They told us you died having Rhonda.]*

SHE: Ain't you still a kid?

TANYA: J'me sens plus comme un cadavre. *[Feel like a cadaver.]*

SHE: . . .

TANYA: J'ai pas mangé de viande séchée depuis que j'ai vécu à la maison. Il est où mon sac à main ? *[Haven't had dried meat since I lived at home. Where's my purse?]*

SHE: Home?

TANYA: Non, j'voulais dire . . . J'sais pas. Pas « la maison ». Ç'a jamais été . . . J'veux dire quand j'vivais avec ma mère. Mais bon, anyway, y'a personne pour s'ennuyer de moi maintenant. Peut-être juste Benty. *[No, I meant . . . I dunno. Not "home." It was never . . . I mean when I lived with my mom. But anyway, nobody to miss me now. Although maybe Benty does.]*

SHE: Benty?

TANYA: Benty le chat. *[Benty the cat.]*

SHE: Oh.

TANYA: Sa queue est restée coincée dans la porte de la voiture, pis elle est jamais revenue droite. *[Her tail got smushed in the car door one time, and it never did straighten back out.]*

TANYA makes a bent tail gesture with her finger.

SHE: What was her name before that?

TANYA: *(hausse les épaules)* J'ai jamais demandé.
[(shrugs) Never asked.]

SHE nods, like she gets it.

T'sais en vrai, quand on y pense, Benty devait tellement être heureuse que tous les humains soient partis, elle s'est sûrement sauvée pour aller mener sa nouvelle vie, faire ce qui lui plaît, partout où ça lui plaît ! Cette viande est tellement fucking bonne ! J'suis mieux d'en garder pour plus tard. Est-ce que t'en gardes pour plus tard ?
[Actually, come to think of it, Benty was probably so excited that all the humans went away, she likely ran off to have a marvellous life wherever the hell she pleased. This meat is fucking yum! I better save some for later. Are you saving some for later?]

SHE: Yes.

TANYA: Okay. Moi, aussi.
[Okay. Me, too.]

SHE: Are you Tanya from Flin Flon born in 1952?

ANCESTOR: Eya.
[Yes.]

TANYA: Ouais. Je suis Lion. Comme si tu pouvais pas le deviner. Toi t'es quoi ?
[Yeah. I'm a Leo. As if you couldn't tell. What are you?]

SHE: Oh, I'm fine. Mostly just . . . walking.

TANYA: Doit être Scorpion.
[Must be a Scorpio.]

SHE smiles.

Je le savais ! On est en dehors de la ville ?
[I knew it! We outside the city?]

SHE: Bout an hour, hour-and-a-half walk outta town. Downriver.

TANYA: Shit.

SHE: Yeah.

TANYA: Où est tout le monde ?
[Where is everybody?]

SHE: That's what I'm trying to find out. Who's left. Or who . . . is me.

TANYA: J'comprends pas.
[I don't get it.]

SHE: I found a woman called Lisa, but she had to go.

TANYA: Où ?
[Where?]

SHE: I think back to her ancestors. She needed to know her real story ending.

TANYA: Comme . . . elle est morte ?
[Like . . . she died?]

SHE: She died a while ago.

ANCESTOR: Ayii dash gaawiin gwayak gii-giiwewinaasii. Gegiin sago.
[But she hadn't properly been sent home. Same as you.]

TANYA: Et tu l'as aidé avec ça ?
[And you helped her out with that?]

Simultaneously:

SHE: I'm not sure.

ANCESTOR: Gigii-doodaamin.
[We did.]

TANYA: Okay. Tu es une Scorpion et ton amie s'appelle Lisa.
[You're a Scorpio and your friend's name is Lisa.]

SHE: My friend's name is Lisa. And she had a great-auntie who she called Grannie Mags whose sister was called Ohna.

TANYA: Attends là. Pourquoi tu me ramènes toujours cette histoire ? En quoi ça me concerne, what the fuck?
[Wait, hold on. Why do you keep bringing them up? What the fuck does that have to do with me?]

SHE: I was just letting you know what I've been doing lately, you don't have to get angry or—

TANYA: Juste—shut up! Qu'est-ce qui se passe ? Avec moi ? Qu'est-ce que tu sais de moi ?
[Just—shut up! What's going on? With me? What do you know about me?]

SHE: Last seen in a dark denim skirt and a pale-yellow sweater. Carrying a purple fringe purse and driving a light-blue two-door Impala.

That is what TANYA is wearing, but without the purse.

TANYA: Okay. Hum. Mon tour. *(observant SHE)* Toi, tu as . . .
[Um. My turn. (assessing SHE) You are . . .]

ANCESTOR: Minwaadizin.
[Be nice.]

TANYA: Été vue pour la dernière fois portant . . . peut-être . . . des parois de tente déchirées et un vieux pantalon de cowboy en cuir. Un drôle de petit chestpad et j'imagine des bottes style faites . . . maison.
[Last seen wearing . . . maybe . . . some ripped-up tent walls and old leathery kinda cowboy pants. Funny little umpire's pad, and I guess home-made sort of . . . boots.]

SHE: I also have some hooks.

TANYA: Hein ?

SHE: It used to have a boat.

TANYA: Groovy.

SHE: "Groovy." Like a path. I like that.

TANYA: Ouais, j'me suis dit que tu apprécierais.
[Yeah, I thought you might.]

SHE: I don't think you have TB.

TANYA: Groovy. C'est quoi toute cette boue ?
[What's with the muck?]

SHE: It's how it is now. Used to be the river.

TANYA: Fuck.

SHE: Yeah. You have to collect water very carefully when you find it. Here.

SHE hands TANYA some water.

TANYA: Wah. T'es super nice.
[Whoa. You're super nice.]

SHE: Oh!

TANYA: J'suis surprise que t'as pas plus d'amis.
[I'm surprised you don't have more friends.]

TANYA drinks.

Tout ça c'est assez trippy. On est en quelle année ?
[Everything is all trippy. What year is it?]

SHE: My best guess is twenty-five After Frederick.

TANYA: Je comprends pas.
[I don't get it.]

SHE: Oh. It's been twenty-five years since Hurricane Frederick. And that was the latest one, so twenty-five After Frederick. Um, for you it's . . . Tanya. Flin Flon. Born 1952, last seen in '71 . . . it is . . . okay . . .

SHE starts counting decades on her hands.

Seventy-one, eighty-one, ninety-one, two thousand one, two thousand eleven, two thousand—

TANYA: Wah, wah, wah ! « Deux mille onze »?
[Whoa, whoa, whoa! "Two thousand eleven"?]

SHE nods still counting on her fingers.

SHE: Two thousand twenty-one, two thousand thirty-one—

TANYA: Attends ! Pourquoi t'as dit « vue pour la dernière fois » à propos de moi ?
[Wait! Why did you say "last seen" about me?]

SHE: In 1971. Yes. You were reported missing. But you were taken into care in 1957.

ANCESTOR: Apii gimaamaa gaa-nibod.
[When your mom passed.]

TANYA: Quand j'avais cinq ans.
[When I was five.]

SHE: Young.

TANYA: En années.
[In years.]

SHE: Yeah.

TANYA: J'me sentais comme un cadavre.
[Felt like a cadaver.]

ANCESTOR: Gisayeyinaan.
[Brother.]

SHE: Your uncle had repeatedly abused you. Beat you within an / inch of your death.

TANYA: Deux doigts de ma vie.
[Inch of my life.]

SHE: Yeah.

TANYA: Ma mère a survécu à tellement de choses. Puis elle nous a plongés en plein milieu de l'enfer. Fucking Flin Flon. Puis, bien sûr, le diable en personne a déménagé là-bas lui avec.
[My mom survived so much. Then she put us right smack dab into the middle of hell. Fucking Flin Flon. And then, of course, the devil himself moved there too.]

ANCESTOR covers her face in sorrow.

SHE: I'm sorry.

TANYA: Est-ce que c'est de ta faute à quel'que part ?
[Is it your fault somehow?]

SHE: Well, it's everyone's fault who didn't stop it. If I had somehow known . . . I dunno.

TANYA: Tu en sais plus sur moi que tu en sais sur toi.
[You know more about me than you do about you.]

SHE: I dunno.

TANYA: Tu viens d'où ?
[Where you from?]

SHE: That way. I walked here.

TANYA: T'as vu ma voiture ?
[Did you see my car?]

SHE: We don't have those anymore.

TANYA: C'est pour ça que tu marchais.
[S'why you walked.]

SHE: I think I would have anyway. It's one of my best things.

TANYA: Groovy.

SHE: Groovy.

TANYA: J'aimais tellement conduire. J'ai jamais eu de permis, mais j'conduisais depuis que j'avais douze ans. J'étais une fantastique conductrice !
[Driving was one of my best things. I never had a licence, but I been driving since I was twelve. I was fantastic at it.]

SHE: It's nice to be good at something.

TANYA: Vraiment. T'as vu mon oncle ?
[It really is. Did you see my uncle?]

SHE: We don't have those anymore either.

TANYA: Pis mon sac à main ?
[How 'bout my purse?]

SHE: Not yet, no.

TANYA: Ça doit être pas loin à que'que part.
[Must be around here somewhere.]

SHE: You know a lot about your own story.

TANYA: Crois-moi, c'est vraiment pas un conte de fées. How do I look?
[Believe me, it's no fairy tale.]

SHE: With your eyes.

SHE laughs.

TANYA: Tu m'fais rire. J'ai un p'tit miroir dans mon sac. Tu le vois nulle part ?
[You're a trip. I have a compact in my purse. Can you see it anywhere?]

SHE: Should we check over there?

SHE motions to where she found TANYA.

TANYA: J'vais aller voir là-bas. Tu peux checker partout ailleurs. C'est mauve. Avec des franges.
[I'll check there. You check everywhere else. It's purple. With fringe.]

SHE: Yes!

SHE starts slowly stepping outward from where they stand, in a spiral.

TANYA: Fuck, t'sais ? J'viens d'avoir cette voiture-là. Je l'ai gagné fair and fucking square! Un jeu d'endurance. J'ai enfin eu mon propre char pis y'a disparu. Ou c'est moi qui ai disparu ? Ou les deux. Mon jour de chance !
[Fuck, you know? I just got that car. Won it fair and fucking square. Endurance game. Finally got my own ride and it goes missing. Or I'm missing? Or both. Just exactly my luck!]

SHE: Some people have all the luck.

TANYA: Exact ! La bonne et la mauvaise. J'ai littéralement les deux. Tout le temps. Mais surtout une chance assez terrible. *(en référence à sa situation)* Dah.
[Exactly! Good and bad. I literally have all of it. All the time. But mostly awful luck. (referencing her situation) Duh.]

TANYA digs in the soil.

J'suis en train de suer ma vie là, ici.
[I'm brewing up some major sweat here.]

SHE hands TANYA her water again.

SHE: Yes, it's very hot now. Except for when it's very cold.

TANYA: On est quel mois là ?
[What month is it?]

SHE: Um. Snow and ice for only three moon cycles. Then the fires. Which don't last long, because there's not much left to burn.

TANYA: Wow. Les scientifiques avaient raison.
[The scientists were right.]

SHE: Elders.

TANYA: C'est sûr ! On est toujours les premiers à le dire, mais est-ce qu'ils écoutent ?
[Of course! We're always the first to say it, but do they listen?]

SHE: No.

TANYA: C'est fucking sûr qu'ils le font pas. Good job, les humains.
[Fuckin' sure they don't. Good job, humans.]

SHE: Fuck!

TANYA: Alors, dis-moi comment tu sais tout ça sur moi.
[So, tell me how you know all that stuff about me.]

SHE: It's written down. Right over there! Lisa collected it and her Grannie Mags saved it.

TANYA: Où ?
[Where?]

SHE: In the ground. But now it's on the ground. See?

SHE shows TANYA the tin can and the scattering of documents. SHE hands TANYA the can and starts stuffing pages into it.

We had it all nice, but then I wrecked it.

TANYA: Tout ça c'est à propos de moi ?
[This is all about me?]

SHE: Well, not just you. There's lots of peoples' stories in here. Unfinished stories. They did a big report about it. Families and friends told about their missing women and girls. Lisa was gathering up all the cases that are connected.

TANYA drops the tin like it's hot.

TANYA: Qui . . . ? Est-ce que c'est dit là-dedans qui a parlé de moi ? Qui m'a « vue pour la dernière fois »?
[Who . . . ? Does it say in there who told about me? Who "last seen" me?]

SHE: Your cousin Tyler.

TANYA: Dis-leur Tyler. C'est lui qui m'a parlé de mon oncle/père. C'est aussi son père. Cela fait de lui mon frère-cousin. J'aimais ce Ty-guy. D'une manière saine. Évidemment. On était pas tous incestueux.
[Tell-all Tyler. He's the one who told me about my uncle/dad. That's his dad, too. So that makes him my brother/cousin. I loved that Ty guy. Like, in a healthy way. Obviously. We weren't all incestors.]

SHE: That's good.

TANYA: Alors, si j'ai été « vue pour la dernière fois » en '71, je suis quoi maintenant ?
[So, if I was "last seen" in '71, what am I now?]

SHE: Um . . .

TANYA stops digging and looks at SHE, who is still spiralling in search of the purse.

TANYA: Tu me vois ou pas ?
[Do you see me or not?]

SHE: I do.

TANYA: Okay, donc je suis pas « vue pour la dernière fois » en '71.
[Okay, so I'm not "last seen" in '71.]

SHE: That's a good point.

TANYA: C'est sûr ! Donc, d'accord. Et. S'il y a autant de personnes disparues qu'ils en ont fait un grand rapport, pourquoi tu t'souviens spécifiquement de moi ? Est-ce que tu es ma vraie tante ?
[Of course! So, okay. And. If there's so many missing people that they did a big report, why do you specifically remember me? Are you my actual auntie?]

ANCESTOR: Gidinawemaaganiwimin.
[(to TANYA) We're family.]

SHE: I remember every story that visits me.

TANYA: Tu le penses vraiment, n'est-ce pas ?
[You really mean that, don't you?]

SHE: Yes.

TANYA: You're a real trip. Tu m'fais trop rire.
[You make me laugh.]

SHE: Thank you.

TANYA: J'ai l'impression qu'on se connaît peut-être.
[Feels like maybe we know each other.]

SHE: We do now!

TANYA: T'as de la chance ! Alors, mais . . . Je suis née en '52 et tu te rappelles de 2031. C'est bien ce que tu dis ?
[Lucky you! So, but . . . I was born in '52 and you remember 2031. Is that what you're saying?]

SHE: Yes.

TANYA: Mais nous voilà . . . J'veux dire . . . le monde est un feu de forêt à la base. La rivière est un bourbier qui pue. Mais nous sommes toutes les deux ici. C'est clair que j'ai pas cent ans. J'veux dire . . . fuck ! J'me sens pas morte.
[But here we are . . . I mean . . . the world is basically a bushfire. The river is a stinking slough. But we're both here. I am obviously not a hundred years old. I mean . . . fuck! I don't feel dead.]

SHE: I'm not sure how to tell if something is alive or dead.

TANYA: Tu disais que ton amie Lisa était morte. Ou que tu l'as tuée. « Retournée vers les ancêtres ».
[You said your friend Lisa's dead. Or you killed her. "Back to the ancestors."]

SHE: Definitely I have never killed any person.

TANYA: Fuck, je l'sais pas. Est-ce que je le sais ?
[Fuck. I dunno, do I?]

SHE: I guess not.

Beat.

TANYA: Comment tu disais que tu t'appelais ?
[What did you say your name was?]

SHE: When?

TANYA: C'est vrai. Trip. Sac à main ! Continue à chercher.
[Right. Trip. Purse! Keep looking.]

TANYA finds something in the dirt.

Holy fuck! Regarde! C'est mon lip gloss préféré!
[Look! It's my favourite lip gloss!]

SHE opens it, or tries to.

Huh. C'est pas normal. On dirait un corn dog. Sûrement faite avec les mêmes ingrédients.
[Ugh. That ain't right. Looks like a corn dog. Probably made of the same stuff.]

SHE: What's a corn dog?

TANYA: C'est bizarre parce que c'est censé être dans mon sac à main. Il doit être ici.
[This is weird because this is supposed to be in my purse. It's gotta be here.]

SHE finds something and holds it up.

SHE: Are these yours?

TANYA: Fuck! C'est ça qui arrive aux Tic Tacs quand ils sont enterrés un milliard d'années ?
[That's what happens to Tic Tacs when they been buried for a billion years?]

SHE: What are they supposed to look like?

TANYA: Ils n'ont pas changé d'un poil.
[They haven't changed one bit.]

TANYA shakes the container of candy so it rattles.

SHE: There's a purplish something here.

TANYA: C'est mon sac ! RIGHT ONNNNN!!!!!!!
[It's my purse! RIGHT ONNNNN!!!!!!!]

SHE: Right in. The dirt.

SHE laughs to herself.

TANYA: Trip, check ça. Waouh . . . J'aurais pas pensé que le faux cuir pouvait pourrir à ce point.
[Trip, look at this. Whoa. I would not have thought fake leather could rot this much.]

SHE: Below certain temperatures it just cracks.

TANYA: Fuck, j'savais qu'elles étaient là !
[Fuck, I knew they were in here!]

TANYA holds up a set of keys.

J'savais que je les avais avec moi. J'ai verrouillé la voiture. Je l'ai faite. C'était safe.
[I knew I had them with me. I locked the car. I did. It was safe.]

SHE: You planning to find your car?

TANYA: Je dois le faire. Il y a quelque chose là-dedans.
[I have to. There's something in there.]

SHE: That's lots of keys for one car.

TANYA: C'mon, Trip. On va parler et marcher.
[Talking and walking.]

SHE: Oh.

They walk.

Are you calling me "Trip"?

TANYA: L'essayer, c'est l'adopter. T'en penses quoi ?
[Trying it out. Whaddaya think?]

SHE: "Trip." Yeah. I can be Trip. Thank you.

TANYA: Un plaisir pour moi. Donc, tu vois ça ? Dans chaque nouvelle famille d'accueil qu'on me mettait, j'allais faire un double des clés en cachette. Juste au cas où ils essaieraient de me jeter dehors. S'ils essayaient de le faire, j'pouvais retourner en dedans et foutre le bordel dans leur maison, ce qui est vraiment très Cancer de ma part.
[My pleasure. So, see these? Every new foster they put me in, I would go cut a spare key on the sly. Just in case they tried kicking me out. If they tried that, I could get back in and fuck up their shit, which is very Cancer cusp of me.]

TRIP: You're inventive.

TANYA: Et passionnée ! Dans ma dernière famille, ils étaient jamais là. Pis ils gardaient leur nourriture dans une armoire barrée. Cheap bastards. J'ai fini par voler la clé de l'armoire à leur fils psychopathe et j'ai fait des copies. Et ça c'est la clé du cadenas que j'ai mis à la porte de la « chambre » qu'ils m'ont donné. À cause de leur fils psychopathe.
[And passionate! My last foster placement, they were never there. And they kept their food locked up. Cheap bastards. Finally stole their sicko son's pantry key and made copies. And this is the key for the padlock I put on the "bedroom" they had me in. Because of their sicko son.]

TRIP: You don't like him?

TANYA: Il m'a genre knocked up.
[He fucking knocked me up.]

TRIP: Knock-out punches?

TANYA: Non, nouille. Knocked up. Il m'a mis enceinte. Ça m'avait pris du temps, t'sais, mais éventuellement j'ai bien vu que j'avais pas mes règles depuis longtemps. J'ai mis le cadenas trop tard.
[No, dum dum. Knocked up me. Pregnant. So, it took me awhile, but eventually I realized I didn't get my period in a long time. I got that lock too late.]

ANCESTOR: Abinoojiiyens Rhonda.
[Baby Rhonda.]

TRIP: Where are we walking?

They stop.

TANYA: Cette clé-là est vraiment vieille. C'est pour la dernière maison où j'ai vécu avec ma mère. On dirait que c'était pas réellement la vraie vie. Toute façon on est pas en train de marcher tout le long jusqu'à Flin Flon, mais si on trouvait une voiture, ce serait une option. Tu vois ? C'est pour ma fucking voiture, que j'ai eu pas longtemps, qui est très importante pour moi pis que j'ai maintenant probablement perdue à tout jamais. Celle-là, ça dit « Le Gold Star Motor Inn ».
[This key is really old. It's for the last house I lived in with my mom. Seems like it was hardly even real life. But anyway, we're not walking all the way to Flin Flon, but if we do find my car, that's an option. See? This is for my fucking car, which I haven't had long and is very important to me and is now, possibly, gone forever. This one says "Gold Star Motor Inn."]

TRIP: What was it like having a mom?

TANYA: Elle était Bélier. Alors. Elle pouvait se battre beaucoup plus que n'importe qui.
[She was an Aries. So. She could fight harder than anyone.]

TRIP: I'm sorry that she had to.

TANYA: Moi aussi.
[Me too.]

Some silence.
ANCESTOR begins a slow grieving dance.

Elle s'appelait Ramona. Les gens l'appelaient Ohna. Moi je l'appelais maman. Dah. Elle est retournée dans « sa communauté » quand elle avait vingt ans. J'sais pas pourquoi. Elle l'a jamais dit. Et sa grande sœur Margaret était devenue la mère de toulemonde. Ma mère aimait jamais se faire dire quoi faire, aussi. Elle s'est fait mettre enceinte—par son fucking horrible frère—pis elle a dit qu'au moment même où j'ai commencé à marcher pis à parler, on est parti. Autrement Matante Maggie m'aurait traité comme si j'étais sa fille.
[Her name was Ramona. People called her Ohna. I called her Mom. Duh. She went back to her "home community" when she was twenty. I dunno why. She never said. And her big sister Margaret was being the mom to the brother and sisters that were still kids. Some of their kids, too. My mom never liked being told what to do. So she gets knocked up with me—by her nasty fucking brother—and she said as soon as I could more or less walk and talk, we took off. Otherwise Auntie Maggie woulda treated me like I was hers.]

TRIP: Sounds good.

TANYA: On pourrait le croire.
[You'd think.]

TRIP: You never went back?

TANYA: Rien que pour un court moment, mais je suis partie tout de suite.
[Only for a sec, but then I left right away.]

TRIP: Why?

TANYA: Pourquoi quoi ?
[Why what?]

TRIP: Why did you go back for a sec and leave right away?

TANYA: Hum.

Silence. TANYA considers deeply about how to respond.

J'étais enceinte à cause du psychopathe de la famille d'accueil. Et j'avais peur. Et . . . J'suis une Lion.
[I was pregnant because of this sicko from the foster's. And I was scared. And . . . I'm a Leo.]

TRIP: Duh.

TANYA: C'était presque mon anniversaire. Et . . .
[It was almost my birthday. And . . .]

Beat.

. . . je voulais essayer de passer une belle journée d'anniversaire comme avant. Alors je me suis sauvée de ma fucking famille d'accueil. J'ai fait du stop jusqu'au Nord jusqu'à ma supposée vraie famille. Et je pouvais bien voir que ma Tante Margaret était benne trop bossy. Pis j'pouvais déjà entendre toutes les choses qu'elle allait me dire. « On fume pas »! « On dit pas de gros mots »! « Pourquoi t'as de l'air enceinte »? Touss'que j'étais était mal. J'pouvais le voir.
[. . . I wanted to try to have a good birthday again. So I ran away from the fucking foster's. And I hitched up north to this so-called family of mine. But as soon as I got there I could see it wasn't going to happen. And I could see my Aunty Margaret was way too bossy. And I could just hear all the things she'd boss me about. "No smoking." "No swearing!" "Why do you look pregnant?" Everything I was was bad. I could tell.]

Fai'que j'suis repartie aussi vite pis j'suis retournée dans cette maudite famille d'accueil. Me suis dit que j'allais manger de leur bouffe jusqu'à ce que mon bébé vienne au monde et après on aurait notre propre place, plus tard.
[So I got the hell outta there and went back to that fucking foster home. I was so hungry. Figured I'd keep eating their food until my baby came, then we'd get our own place somehow.]

TRIP: How old were you?

TANYA: Treize ans. Presque quatorze.
[Thirteen. Almost fourteen.]

Silence.

La dernière fois que j'ai eu un gâteau d'anniversaire, je venais d'avoir cinq ans. Un gâteau avec des confettis. Crémage glacé bleu avec des roses roses. On avait invité des enfants du quartier. Mon cousin Ty, c'est sûr. Sa mère. Et puis, hum . . . on avait pas invité mon oncle. Parce que . . .
[The last time I had a birthday cake, I was turning five. Confetti cake. Blue icing with pink roses. We had some kids over from the neighbourhood. My cousin Ty, of course. His mom. And, um . . . we didn't invite my uncle. Because . . .]

TRIP: He was awfully cruel.

TANYA: Yeah. On a fait un gâteau. Pis des cadeaux. On s'en allait sortir dehors pour jouer à des jeux. L'œuf et la cuillère, une course à trois jambes, t'sais ? Des prix et tout ça.
[Yeah. We had done cake. And presents. We were about to go outside and play games. Egg and spoon, three-legged races, y'know? Prizes and everything.]

TRIP nods to keep TANYA talking, though she has no idea what these games are.

Pis le frère de ma mere est apparu. « Ohnaaaaaa ! Fucking bitch! Tu peux pas m'enlever ma fille »! Genre comme, il admettait que j'étais la sienne.
[My mom's brother shows up. "Ohnaaaaa! You fucking bitch! You can't keep my girl from me!" Like, he was admitting I was his.]

Beat.

Ma tante, sa femme ? elle dit « Les enfants vous prenez vos chaussures et venez avec moi ! Tout de suite. J'ai les sacs à surprises. Suivez-moi »! Elle conduit les enfants du côté de la rue, tout le monde courant les chaussures dans leurs mains. Ma mère sort par l'arrière et j'échappe à leur vue. Je reste dans la cuisine, cachée derrière le comptoir, et j'attends que mon oncle s'en aille pour qu'on puisse jouer à nos jeux et gagner nos prix.
[My auntie, his wife? She says, "All you kids grab your shoes and come with me. Now. I have the goodie bags. Follow me!" She leads the kids away and down the street, all running with their shoes in their hands. Mom goes out the back and I slip their notice. I stay in the kitchen, ducked down beside the counter, and wait for my uncle to leave so we can play those games and win those prizes.]

ANCESTOR: Ohn, Tanya . . .
[Oh, Tanya . . .]

TANYA: Il était vraiment énervé et en colère, il allait pas se calmer de sitôt. J'entends son poing se fracasser sur ma mère. Elle s'écrase au sol. Des cris, des coups de pied, des coups de poing. J'sais pas comment qu'un seul corps peut prendre autant de coups. Comment qu'un seul homme peut contenir autant de rage. Je sens de la morve qui coule jusqu'à ma bouche et j'imagine que c'est du sang parce que ma mère saigne. J'entends des sirènes de police au loin qui se rapproche et mon oncle-père trébuche partout en essayant de se ressaisir. Pis il s'enfuit dans la ruelle, j'imagine. La police l'a rattrapé quelques blocs plus loin.
[He was really spazzing, no slowing down in sight. I hear his fist break against my mom. She hits the ground. Screaming. Kicking. Punching.

I dunno how one body can take so much. How one man can hold so much rage. I feel snot run down to my mouth and I think it's blood because my mom is bleeding. I hear sirens far away getting closer and my uncle-dad stumbles around trying to get himself together. And he runs out the back door. Down the alley, I guess. Cops pick him up a few blocks away.]

Je sors de ma cachette, et quand j'suis sûre qu'il est parti, je m'en vais voir ma mère dans l'herbe. J'ai tenu la jambe de Maman parce que c'était la seule chose d'elle qui était pas brisé. Son souffle semblait se noyer. Elle essayait de dire mon nom.
[I creep out of my hiding place, and when I'm sure he's really gone, I go to my mom on the grass. Holding onto Mom's one leg because it was the only part of her not broken. Her breath sounded drowning. She was trying to say my name.]

ANCESTOR: Tanya.

TANYA: Pis je lui ai dit que j'étais ok pis que matante avait sauvé les sacs à surprise.
[And I told her I'm okay and that Auntie saved the goodie bags.]

ANCESTOR: Giinawind gaa-agaashiiwid Tanya.
[Our little Tanya.]

TANYA: La prochaine chose que je réalise, c'est les ambulanciers qui marchaient lentement, vraiment lentement. Alors je m'accroche à ma mère comme si ma vie en dépendait. Je savais qu'ils voulaient me la prendre pour toujours.
[Next thing I realize is ambulance people walking towards us slow slow slow. So I'm clinging to my mom for dear life. I knew they wanted to take her away from me forever.]

TRIP: The ambulance people?

TANYA: Quelqu'un comme ça. Des gens en uniforme. Je me souviens qu'ils arrivaient pas à me faire lâcher Maman. J'me suis battue comme elle.
[Someone like that. Uniforms people. I remember they couldn't make me let go of Mom. I fought like her.]

Et le moment d'après j'étais réveillée et toute seule dans un grand lit blanc dans une chambre vert vomi.
[And the next thing I knew I was awake and all by myself in an all-white bed in a puke-green room.]

TRIP: And your mom?

TANYA: Ils ont dit que j'allais être en famille d'accueil maintenant.
[They said I was a foster kid now.]

ANCESTOR: Ishkwaaj gaagii-ikidod giwiinzowin.
[The last word she said was your name.]

TANYA: Je dois trouver mon sac à main.
[I need to find my purse.]

TRIP: You have it.

TANYA: Oui. C'est vrai.
[Yeah. Right.]

Beat.

Si tu m'as trouvée, peut-être que je vais la trouver. Et si je trouve mes bébés filles . . .
[If you found me, maybe I'll find her. And if I find my baby girls . . .]

ANCESTOR: Ikwezensag?
[Girls?]

TRIP: Girls, plural?

TANYA: . . . peut-être que j'peux avoir quelqu'un, dans ce maudit monde atroce, qui peut être tout à moi.
[. . . maybe there can be someone in this ugly goddamn world who can be all mine.]

ANCESTOR: Niinawind giin.
[We're yours.]

TRIP: Your baby from the sicko? And . . . ?

TANYA: Ils l'ont pris. Ils m'ont assommée à l'hôpital pis elle . . .
[They took her. They knocked me out in the hospital and she . . .]

ANCESTOR: Gii-gimoodiwag.
[Was stolen.]

TANYA: J'allais avoir quelqu'un, dans ce maudit monde atroce, qui allait être tout à moi.
[There was finally gonna be someone in this ugly goddamn world who was gonna be all mine.]

ANCESTOR: Ogii-izhinizhaawaan ji-bi-wiijiiyaamid.
[They sent her to live with me.]

TANYA: Que je pouvais aimer, qui pouvait peut-être m'aimer, et de qui je serais folle, tu comprends? Tout ce que j'allais avoir à faire à partir de là c'était de prendre soin de cette petite. La garder en sécurité.
[Who I could love, who might love me, and who I'd be all about, you know? All I would ever have to do from now on was look after that little one. Keep her safe.]

ANCESTOR: Ningii-wiidamaagoomin egii-niboyan.
[They told us you had died having her.]

TANYA: M'assurer qu'elle allait avoir une meilleure vie que la mienne—ce qui serait pas très difficile, les standards étant vraiment fucking low. Et je savais que je pouvais y arriver.
[Make sure she had a better life than me—which wouldn't be too hard, standards were pretty goddamn fucking low. And I knew I could do it.]

ANCESTOR: Geget igo gigashkitoon.
[Of course you could.]

TANYA: Mais ils l'ont volée.
[But they stole her.]

ANCESTOR: Rhonda gii-izhinikaazo.
[Her name was Rhonda.]

TRIP: Margaret. Ramona Ohna. Tanya. Rhonda. Lisa.

TANYA: Ils m'ont dit qu'elle a jamais existé. Ils m'ont endormie pis ils m'ont opérée pis m'ont dit qu'elle a jamais été là. Ils ont essayé de remplir mon espace vide avec leurs mensonges, m'ont dit que c'était une tumeur horrible et pas une petite fille, mais t'sais, je savais. Ils m'ont dit qu'ils ont sauvé ma vie en m'opérant.
[They said she never existed. They put me to sleep and cut me up and told me she never was. Tried to fill my empty space up with lies. Said it was a terrible tumour and not a baby girl, like I knew. Said they saved my life by cutting it out.]

ANCESTOR: Ninzaagii-aayens Tanya.
[My sweet Tanya.]

TANYA: C'qui fait que j'me suis sauvée de ce petit hôpital de merde pour m'en aller à la ville et suis devenue invisible—ils pouvaient pas. Me. Trouver. J'suis sûre que ma fille, ma bébé fille, s'est fait vendre à un petit couple de blancs parce qu'elle ressemblait tellement au petit blanc qui avait forcé la porte de mon propre corps. Encore et encore. Je l'ai cherchée partout. Je la voyais partout sans jamais pouvoir la

tenir, même pas une fois. Et cette ville m'a fait mal jusqu'à me mener à deux doigts de la mort. Un loup est venu. Il pouvait sentir le sang.
[So I ran from that shitty small-town hospital to the city and became invisible—they could. Not. Find me. Bet my girl, my baby girl, got sold to some white couple 'cause she came out looking so much like the white boy who forced me outside my own body. Again and again. Looked for her everywhere. Seeing her everywhere and never holding her, not once. And that city beat me within an inch of my death. Then a wolf came along. He could smell the blood.]

TRIP: Wolves lasted a long time.

TANYA: Pis il m'a dit qu'il pouvait me montrer le chemin. Et j'avais tellement faim que je l'ai suivi. Tout le long jusqu'au Gold Star Motor Inn. Il m'a mis dans une chambre spéciale pour les grandes filles loin de chez elles. Avec un lit spécial avec bon nombre de visiteurs et une porte tournante. Et les visiteurs forçaient la porte de mon corps encore et encore. L'un après l'autre après l'autre.
[And he said he'd show me the way. And I was so starved that I followed. All the way to the Gold Star Motor Inn. He put me in a special room for big girls far from home. With a special bed with lots of visitors and a rotating door. And the visitors forced me out of my body again and again. One after another after another.]

ANCESTOR: Gaa-baazhkiziged anang.
[Shooting star.]

TANYA: Ça veut dire quoi, « vue pour la dernière fois »?
[What does it mean, "last seen?"]

TRIP: I see you. You can't be last seen. We're here now.

TANYA: Le Gold Star Motor Inn attirait les loups.
[The Gold Star Motor Inn attracted wolves.]

TRIP: But only on the ground.

TANYA: Ils venaient de partout des milles à la ronde.
[They came from miles around.]

TANYA trembles with fear. TRIP gathers her up and offers a new ending.

TRIP: So one day, you rose. Up until then the sky had cycled through its colours like always. Breaking morning soft pinks and oranges. Pale blue. Bright blue. Richer, deeper hue, pinks and purples and dark blue. Blue black. Blue black with bright snips for stars. A holy quilt your grannies made. And then something happened. The earth shook the bright snips loose and fire rained down on every sister. One. Two. Three. Four. Five. Six. Seven. Eight. And the fires burned and the smoke went up and so did you. Up, up up to all the aunties and sisters and moms and daughters. Sparkle shine time.

TANYA: Et puis j'suis redescendue. De quel côté Lisa est partie ?
[And then I came back down. Which way did Lisa go?]

TRIP: That way.

TANYA: D'accord. Parfait. Bon, ben je vais aller de ce côté-là aussi.
[Right. Okay. Well then I'll go that way, too.]

TRIP takes some tobacco from her bundle.

TRIP: Take some of this. And this!

TRIP gives TANYA a candy bar.

TANYA: Wow.

TRIP: Lisa said you have to make offerings. So . . . Save some for your family.

TANYA: J'vais faire ça.
[I will.]

TRIP: Groovy.

TANYA: Prends ça ! Porte-le autour de ton cou. Comme ça on va se connaître la prochaine fois.
[Take this! Wear it around your neck. So that we know each other next time.]

> *TANYA takes the motel key off the ring and gives it to TRIP. TRIP releases a leather string from somewhere on her person and ties it around her neck with the key dangling.*

TRIP: We know each other forever. You gave me my name. Like a mom can do.

TANYA: J'pourrais être ta maman.
[I could be your mom.]

TRIP: Really?

ANCESTOR: Geget.
[Really.]

TANYA: Je sais pas.
[I don't know.]

TRIP: It's okay. We can still be auntie and niece.

TANYA: Matante Trip.
[Auntie Trip.]

TRIP: Sounds good.

TANYA: À plus tard, Matante Trip.
[See you later, Auntie Trip.]

TRIP: See you later, niece Tanya.

TANYA: Les gens disent pas vraiment « niece » pis « le nom ». C'est soit juste « niece », soit juste le nom.
[People don't really say "niece" then "name." It's either just "niece" or just their name.]

TRIP: Okay. Thank you, niece.

TANYA: Merci, Matante. Un câlin vite vite !
[Thanks, Auntie. Quick hug!]

TANYA hugs TRIP. TRIP finds herself hugging TANYA back quite strongly.

Bye Matante Trip.
[Bye Auntie Trip.]

TRIP: Bye. Niece.

Beat.

Tanya.

As TANYA walks away, TRIP closes her eyes.
TANYA hangs her clothes in the trees, like the Red Dresses. She leaves.

Lisa. Lisa's great-great-aunt is Margaret: Grannie Mags. Lisa's great-grandma is Ramona. Ramona and Margaret are sisters. Ramona was Tanya's mom. Lisa's mom, raised up by Grannie Mags, is Rhonda. Rhonda disappeared. And Rhonda's mom?

ANCESTOR: Tanya awe. Ganoonzh. Ganoonzh ji-bi-azhegiiwed!
[It's Tanya. Call her. Call her back!]

TRIP: I'm missing you, Tanya.

ANCESTOR: Tanya!

TRIP: Don't leave me here.

Beat.

I walk. I'm okay. I'm Auntie Trip. I have a niece named Tanya. And a friend called Lisa. Aaniin. I'm Trip.

They speak all at once:

ANCESTOR: Trip, daga. Ganoozh Tanya ji-bi-azhegiiwed.
Gaawiin miinawaa gidaa-waniiyaasiinaan.
Ningii-wiindamaagoo egii-nibod.
Ganoonzh ji-bi-azhegiiwed.
Wiindamaw egii-ombigi'ag odaanisan.
Rhonda gii-izhinikaazo. Lisa omaamaayan. Daga.
TANYA! RHONDA! RHONDAAAA!

[Trip, please. Call Tanya back.
We can't lose her again.
They'd told me she died.
Call her back.
Tell her I raised her daughter.
Her name was Rhonda. She's Lisa's mother. Please.
TANYA! RHONDA! RHONDAAAA!]

TRIP, under ANCESTOR's pleas, repeats the names of people she has met.

TRIP: Auntie Trip. Niece Tanya. Friend Lisa. Grannie Mags.
Ramona Ohna.
Auntie Trip. Niece Tanya. Friend Lisa. Grannie Mags. Ramona Ohna.
Auntie Trip. Niece Tanya. Friend Lisa. Grannie Mags. Ramona Ohna.
Auntie Trip. Niece Tanya. Friend Lisa. Grannie Mags. Ramona Ohna.

ANCESTOR cries.

The trickle of water increases.
TRIP sees this.
She goes to the water and touches it.

Water. WATEEERRRRRR!

TRIP rushes about, thrilled by the running water.

4. FREEZING / MASHKAWAAKWADIN / GEL

TRIP trips on a woman buried in the dirt. The woman barely sounds her words.

WOMAN: De l'eau ! De l'eau !
[Water. Water!]

TRIP: Oh holy hell, holy heck! I gotcha.

TRIP quickly, furiously unearths the woman with her hands.

ANCESTOR: Rhonda.

TRIP: It's okay. You're okay. Picture a blue sky.

WOMAN: Le ciel bleu.
[Blue sky.]

TRIP hands the WOMAN her water. The WOMAN sips very slightly.

TRIP: And . . . ripe berries.

WOMAN: Okay. Okay.

TRIP: Um. Fresh pickerel. The bleach and sunshine clean of Gran's tea towels.

WOMAN: Quo . . . ?
[Wha . . . ?]

TRIP: It's okay. Keep breathing. You're okay.

WOMAN: Je suis complètement gelée. J'ai l'impression d'avoir de la glace dans mes côtes. L'air peut pas entrer.
[I'm freezing hot. Feels like ice in my ribs. Air can't get in.]

TRIP: It's changed.

WOMAN: Pour vrai ?
[Is has?]

TRIP: Yes. It's thick everywhere now. All the time.

WOMAN: Terrible.
[Awful.]

TRIP: I'm so sorry.

WOMAN: Qui es-tu ?
[Who are you?]

TRIP: Oh. Me? My name is Trip. I have a friend named Lisa and my niece is called Tanya from Flin Flon. She gave me my name. I'm . . . I'm a carrier. And a finder.

WOMAN: Finders keepers?

TRIP: No.

WOMAN: Okay.

TRIP: Are you okay now?

WOMAN: De mieux en mieux, pour l'instant. J'sais pas.
[Good as it gets, for now. I dunno.]

TRIP: You might not be alive.

WOMAN: Quoi ?
[What?]

TRIP: I just don't want you to get your hopes up.

WOMAN: Ben, merci.
[Well . . . thank you very much.]

TRIP: Okay.

WOMAN: Si j'suis pas en vie, ça fait quoi de toi ?
[If I'm not alive, what does that make you?]

TRIP: Nobody ever asked me that.

WOMAN: Et maintenant ?
[So now what?]

TRIP: Last two times they had to go. Find some things on their own. So . . . what do you want to do?

WOMAN: Ben . . . qu'est-ce qui reste ?
[Well . . . what's left?]

TRIP: I don't know what to say. This is the most people I've seen in forever.

WOMAN looks around at the empty space.

There were those other two. And everyone seems to have strong feelings about Flin Flon. And . . . and you. Would you like some dried moose meat?

WOMAN: J'veux pas aller à goddamn Flin Flon !
[I don't wanna go to goddamn Flin Flon!]

TRIP: Then you won't!

WOMAN: Ben, je suis qui ? J'ferme les yeux et tout est plus blanc que blanc.
[Well, who am I? Close my eyes and it's just snow-blind nothing.]

TRIP: We can try to figure it out together.

WOMAN: Tu parles toujours comme un boy scout ou quoi ?
[Are you a damn boy scout or what?]

TRIP: I'm pretty sure we don't have those anymore.

> *The WOMAN has a bout of rather hysterical laughter. TRIP does not join her.*

WOMAN: Holy shit.

TRIP: Your laugh didn't sound happy.

WOMAN: Qui. Es-tu ?
[Who. Are you?]

TRIP: Trip.

WOMAN: Ok. Tu viens d'où ?
[Okay. Where you from?]

TRIP: My people have always been here.

WOMAN: D'accord. Maintenant, on arrive à quelque chose. C'est la même chose pour moi.
[Okay. Now we're getting somewhere. That's the same for me.]

TRIP: Great! What else do you know?

WOMAN: Donne-moi un sujet.
[Gimme a topic.]

TRIP: You.

WOMAN: Je suis là. C'est mon corps. Je sais c'est quoi un ciel bleu. Des baies. Du pickerel frais. Ce sont des arbres. En quelque sorte. Tu t'appelles Trip. Tu connais quelqu'un qui s'appelle « Lisa ». Quelqu'un qui s'appelle « Tanya ». Flin Flon est un gros non. Et l'air a déjà été . . . meilleur.
[I'm here. This is my body. I know what blue sky is. Berries. River-fresh pickerel. These are trees. Kinda. Your name is Trip. You know someone named "Lisa." Someone called "Tanya." Flin Flon is a hell no. And the air used to be . . . better.]

TRIP: And we come from here.

WOMAN: Pour tout le bien que ça nous fait.
[For all the good it's doing us.]

TRIP: Would walking help?

WOMAN: Aiderait quoi ?
[Help what?]

TRIP: Anything.

WOMAN: Je sens que ma jambe est un peu gelée.
[My legs feel a little frozen.]

TRIP: Makes sense.

Beat.

I usually walk.

WOMAN: Ouais, je . . . je sens que c'est marcher qui m'a d'abord amenée ici.
[Yeah, I . . . I feel like walking is what got me here in the first place.]

TRIP: I can sit with you.

TRIP sits, not close to WOMAN at all.

WOMAN: J'avais besoin d'aide.
[I needed some help.]

ANCESTOR: Geget igo. Ozhaawashko-giizhigong. Aditegin miinan. Biinaagami-ziibi ogaans!
[Of course. Blue sky. Ripe berries. Fresh pickerel.]

WOMAN: Je sens que j'ai besoin d'une . . . t'as une cigarette ? Hey—je fume ! C'est un autre indice.
[I feel like I need a . . . you got a smoke? Hey—I smoke! That's another clue.]

TRIP: I have tobacco.

ANCESTOR: Eya.
[Yes.]

WOMAN: Et du papier.
[And papers?]

TRIP: There's some over there.

WOMAN: Oh, c'est correct.
[Aw, that's okay.]

TRIP hands the woman some tobacco.

Simultaneously:

ANCESTOR: Ozhaawashko-giizhigong. Aditegin miinan. Biinaagamiziibi ogaans!
[Blue sky. Ripe berries. Fresh pickerel . . .]

WOMAN: Ciel Bleu. Baies mûres. Pickerel frais . . .
[Blue sky. Ripe berries. Fresh Pickerel . . .]

TRIP: The bleach and sunshine clean of Gran's tea towels.

WOMAN: Ouais.

The WOMAN smells the tobacco and then holds it to her heart.

Ça me semble familier ?
[This feels familiar?]

WOMAN inhales the tobacco deeply.

Je connais ça.
[I know this.]

After a moment, the WOMAN pulls out a medicine bag from inside her clothing. It is still around her neck.

ANCESTOR: Mashkiki.
[Medicine.]

TRIP: Another clue.

WOMAN: C'est à ma Grams.
[This is my Grams's.]

TRIP: You have a grandma.

WOMAN: La cuisine de Grams. Toute en jaune. Avec des canards blancs. Du thé chaud.
[Grams's kitchen. All yellow. With white ducks. Hot tea.]

TRIP: You are your grandma's girl.

> *The WOMAN nods, full of memory and love.*

WOMAN: Je le suis.
[I am.]

TRIP: *(full of warmth)* That happens a lot.

WOMAN: En vrai elle était la sœur de ma grand-mère, mais ma grand-mère nous avait quitté depuis longtemps. J'ai de la chance que ma Grams m'ait prise sous son aile.
[She was actually my grandma's sister, but my grandma was long gone. Lucky for me Grams took me in.]

TRIP: That happened a lot, too.

> *The WOMAN picks up some soil and holds it to her heart, then puts the soil and tobacco together.*
> *TRIP puts some more food into the soil.*

We seek, we gather, we collect. Water makes for walking.
Stories are for talking. Offering.

> *ANCESTOR stands and enacts the memory with WOMAN, though she appears to WOMAN as in a memory, not yet truly there with her.*

WOMAN: Grams. Elle a dit . . .
[Grams. She said . . .]

ANCESTOR: *(as Grams)* Sors plus avec ces gens encore ce soir, Rhonda.
[Don't be going out with that crowd again tonight, Rhonda.]

RHONDA: Rhonda.

TRIP: Rhonda.

RHONDA: J'serais safe, Grams. J'fais rien de méchant, plus jamais. Juste quelques bières.
[I'll be safe, Grams. I don't do any nasty stuff no more. Just have a couple beers.]

ANCESTOR: *(as Grams)* T'es même pas supposée boire une seule bière.
[You're not supposed to be having even one beer.]

RHONDA: Tu vas même pas me voir boire, Grams. Tu peux dire que tu as fait ta part.
[You won't even see me have it, Grams. You can say you did your part.]

ANCESTOR: *(as Grams)* J'te reconnais plus.
[You're out on my recognitions.]

RHONDA: Tu me relâches plus.
[Recognizance.]

ANCESTOR: *(as Grams)* Tu peux le dire, mais tu n'as pas l'air de savoir ce que ça veut dire.
[Well, you can say it, but you don't seem to know what it means.]

RHONDA: J'rentrerai pas tard, Grams. Lisa dort profondément. Elle a eu ses histoires et un peu de lait chaud.
[I won't be late, Grams. And Lisa is sound asleep. She had her stories and some warm milk.]

ANCESTOR: *(as Grams)* Mets une tuque. Et mes bottes ! Tu peux pas sortir comme ça.
[Wear a toque. And my boots! You can't go out like that.]

RHONDA: T'en fais pas avec ça, Grams !
[Don't worry 'bout it, Grams!]

ANCESTOR: *(as Grams)* Ma fille . . .
[My girl . . .]

RHONDA: J't'aime !
[Love you!]

> *RHONDA leaves the house into the void.*
> *ANCESTOR steps out of the telling.*

ANCESTOR: Gizaagii'in.
[I love you.]

RHONDA: *(à TRIP)* L'instant d'après j'étais dans un bar. Puis un autre. Puis un party. Puis un autre. Après je marchais pour rentrer à la maison. Je devais partir avec mes amies, mais je l'avais pas trouvée.
[(to TRIP) Next thing I was at a bar. And then another. Then a party. Then another. Then I was walking home. Was supposed to leave with my friends but couldn't find them.]

TRIP: What next, Rhonda?

RHONDA: Des lumières tournoient sur la neige. Rouge bleu rouge bleu. Évidemment c'était le même cochon qui me harcèle tout le temps. Lui pis une femme flic. Je leur ai dit que j'avais même pas levé mon pouce—hitching is illegal. Ils ont pas ri. Il a dit . . .
[Lights swirling on snow. Red blue red blue. And of course it was that one pig who always rides my ass. Him and a lady cop. And I told them I didn't even have my thumb out—hitching is illegal. And they didn't laugh. He said . . .]

> *RHONDA brings TRIP to the telling, then TRIP speaks the voice of the police. ANCESTOR walks a circle around this telling.*

TRIP: *(as cop)* We'll take you right home. No need to call this in if you co-operate.

RHONDA: J'suis presque à la maison anyway.
[I'm almost home anyways.]

TRIP: *(as cop)* Get in the car.

RHONDA: C'est juste à trois blocs d'ici.
[It's only three more blocks.]

TRIP: *(as cop)* It's thirty-five below. And you're out past curfew. We can call your PO or you can get in the car.

RHONDA and TRIP end the telling as ANCESTOR stands with them.

RHONDA: Pis sa partner disait rien. Mais elle m'a regardé droit dans les yeux. Donc j'ai embarqué.
[And his partner didn't say anything. But she looked me right in the eye. And so I got in.]

ANCESTOR: Gii-gimoodiwag
[Stolen.]

RHONDA: Ils ont conduit, conduit.
[They drove and drove.]

TRIP: And then they stopped.

RHONDA: Pis ils ont pris mon manteau.
[And they took my coat.]

TRIP: And your shoes.

ANCESTOR: Gaawiin gegoo wiiyakwaan.
[No toque.]

TRIP: And it was thirty-six below.

ANCESTOR: Ninaagadendam giishpin ji-gimoodiwaadimban gitaadizii-wikwe makizinan.
[I wonder if they woulda stolen an old woman's boots.]

TRIP: If they woulda felt her miles.

RHONDA: Et ils ont fait demi-tour et sont partis.
[And then they turned around and drove away.]

TRIP: Minus thirty-six.

ANCESTOR: Thirty-seven.

TRIP: Thirty-eight.

RHONDA: Le froid qui tue comme un poing dans les poumons.
[Killing cold like a fist in your lungs.]

TRIP: You walked and walked.

RHONDA: Fallait que je m'en retourne pour ma petite.
[Had to get home to my little girl.]

ANCESTOR: Lisa-wens.
[Little Lisa.]

TRIP: But you were so cold.

RHONDA: Tellement fatiguée. J'avais besoin. De dormir un peu.
[So tired. Just needed. A little rest.]

RHONDA slowly lies down on her side, then comes to a stillness.

Pis j'ai eu chaud.
[And then I was warm.]

ANCESTOR: Mikomii-waaboowaanan dedibayii giinawind emaajaayang.
[The ice blankets around us as we go.]

RHONDA: Sommeil de neige.
[Snow sleep.]

Time lands.

Et quoi ensuite ?
[And then what?]

TRIP: Now we're here.

RHONDA: Je peux le sentir, j'suis plus là. Est-ce que ça fait du sens ?
[I can feel me, gone. Does that make sense?]

TRIP nods and reaches a hand out to RHONDA, who takes it.

Tu es froide, aussi.
[You're cold, too.]

TRIP: Yes.

RHONDA: J'veux dire à ma Grams que je suis désolée.
[I wanna tell my Grams I'm sorry.]

ANCESTOR: Wegonen onji?
[What for?]

Beat.

RHONDA: Peut-être que c'est à ça que ça sert les funérailles, han ? Pour que les morts puissent revenir un peu et laissent savoir à tout le monde à quel point ils se sentent coupable.
[Maybe that's what funerals are really for, hey? So the dead can hang around for a sec and let everyone know how sorry they are.]

TRIP: You're not guilty.

RHONDA: La seule souffrance que ma Grams pouvait connaître c'était de me perdre. Pis je suis sortie et je suis allée me perdre.
[The only suffering my Grams coulda known was losing me. And I went and got myself lost.]

ANCESTOR: Gii-gimoodiwag.
[Stolen.]

Beat.

RHONDA: Une chance que je n'ai pas pris ses bottes. Elle les aurait jamais revues. Mais mes pieds . . . mes pieds sont complètement gelés.
[Good thing I didn't take her boots. She never woulda seen them again. But my feet . . . my feet are freezing.]

TRIP takes off her own boots and gives them to RHONDA.

TRIP: Here.

As TRIP puts the boots on RHONDA, RHONDA cries.

RHONDA: Non, non.

TRIP: Would you be interested in having a hug with me?

Beat.

RHONDA: Personne m'a jamais demandé ça avant.
[No one ever asked me that before.]

TRIP: My niece Tanya hugged me, and I think it was very helpful.

Beat. Beat.
They hug, warmly and strong.
TRIP cries.

RHONDA: Pourquoi tu pleures ?
[Whatchoo crying for?]

TRIP: I forgot how much I was lonely.

RHONDA: Arrête ça tout de suite. On a du travail à faire. Il faut qu'on fasse nos funérailles.
[Well, cut it out, man. We got work to do. We gotta have our funerals.]

TRIP: Me, too?

RHONDA: Ben, ce sera quand la prochaine fois que tu auras le temps ?
[Well, when else are you gonna have time?]

TRIP: I am pretty busy walking.

RHONDA: Comment le tien se passe ?
[How does yours go?]

TRIP: Maybe we could sing a song for our funerals.

RHONDA: Tu connais un chant ?
[Do you know a song?]

TRIP starts singing what ANCESTOR sang some time ago.

Je crois que je connais ce chant.
[I think I know this song.]

> RHONDA *then removes the boots and sets them before her, as though they occupy the space saved for her Grams.*

> ANCESTOR *steps into them.*
> RHONDA *and Grams connect.*
> *Under this,* TRIP *sings, with more voices ghosted in.*

Grams. Je m'excuse de pas être rentrée plus tôt. Je m'excuse de pas m'être habillée plus chaudement. J'm'excuse de pas avoir su que j'étais partie . . . avant maintenant.
[Grams. I'm sorry I didn't come home sooner. I'm sorry I didn't dress warmer. I'm sorry I didn't even know I was gone till now.]

ANCESTOR: *(as Grams)* Nous avions perdu ma sœur.
[We lost my sister.]

TRIP: Ramona-Ohna.

ANCESTOR: *(as Grams)* Et puis ta mère.
[And then your mom.]

TRIP: Tanya.

ANCESTOR: *(as Grams)* Ensuite le Créateur t'a donnée à moi.
[Then Creator gave you to me.]

TRIP: Rhonda.

ANCESTOR: *(as Grams)* Et j'ai mis mes deux bras autour de toi et je t'ai jamais lâchée.
[And I put both arms around you and never let go.]

RHONDA: Je me suis toujours sentie soutenue.
[I always felt held.]

ANCESTOR: *(as Grams)* J'aurais dû nous sortir de cette ville affamée.
[I should have moved us far from this hungry city.]

RHONDA: Tu es notre maison.
[You're our home.]

ANCESTOR: *(as Grams)* Quelque soit l'endroit où on se trouve, j'espère que tu peux me pardonner.
[Wherever we are, I hope you can forgive me.]

RHONDA: Tu as rien fait de mal.
[You've done nothing wrong.]

They hug, completing one another. When they step apart:

TRIP: You're going to leave together, and I have to keep walking.

ANCESTOR: Gishiime wa'a.
Gigii-mikawinaan.
Ogii-mikawaan gimaamaayan.

[This is your sister.
She found us.
She found your mother.]

RHONDA: Ils vous ont dit qu'elle est morte en me donnant naissance.
[They told you she'd died having me.]

TRIP: Lisa. Lisa's great-great-aunt is Margaret: Grannie Mags. Lisa's great-great-grandma is Ramona. Ramona and Margaret are sisters. Lisa's mom, raised up by Grannie Mags, is Rhonda. Rhonda disappeared. And Rhonda's mom?

ANCESTOR: Ganoonzh gimaamaa. Gishime onandendaan odibaajimoowin.
[Call your mom. Your sister needs her story.]

TRIP: I have to keep walking.

ANCESTOR: Tanya Flin Flon onjii, gii-nitaawigi 1952. Ishwaaj gii-waabamaa ebiiskang gaa-makadewaanig ogiizhki-goodaaz zhigo babagiwayaaniiginig zhigo waabiyaazaawaanig opagibiinda'oozonim. Ogii-bimiiwidoon miini-miskwaanid zhooniyaawazh, niisiiwezhigaade zhigo gii-bimibizonige waabiyaa-ozhaawashko odaabaan, niizh ishkwaandeman imaa Impala-wing.
[Tanya from Flin Flon, born in 1952. Last seen in a dark denim skirt and a pale-yellow sweater. Carrying a purple fringe purse and driving a light-blue two-door Impala.]

TRIP sings and does not move.
WOMAN finds TANYA's clothing, exchanges them for hers—the start of calling forth TANYA.
ANCESTOR and WOMAN turn the plough over, converting it into a travois.

We hear thunder.

WOMAN and ANCESTOR circle TRIP as they pull the upward facing-plough/travois.
TRIP continues singing.
They all sing together: three languages at once.

TRIP struggles for breath.

ANCESTOR and WOMAN help TRIP onto the travois.

TRIP: There are billions of us. We are the land, the water, and the stars.

ANCESTOR: Gidayaamin.
[We are.]

The two women pull TRIP *onto the travois.*
After a full circle, they travel up the centre.

The loudest crack of thunder or cracking of land stops the singing.
TRIP *sits upright on the travois.*

5. FLOODING / MOOSHKAMONG / INONDATION

TRIP holds up the key TANYA gave her.

TRIP: Tanya. At the Gold Star.

ANCESTOR and WOMAN understand. They step away from TRIP and the travois, making space for ceremony. WOMAN embodies TANYA again.

Simultaneously:

ANCESTOR: Tanya. Ozaawaa Zhooniyaa Anang gabeshiwing imaa. (Gold Star Motor Inn imaa.)
[Tanya. At the Gold Star Motor Inn.]

WOMAN: Tanya. Au Gold Star Motor Inn.
[Tanya. At the Gold Star Motor Inn.]

The three women work together to create the picture/map of what happened on this land, in this river.

TANYA: Ça m'avait pris du temps, t'sais, mais éventuellement j'ai bien vu que j'avais pas mes règles depuis longtemps. J'étais totalement effrayée. La dernière fois que c'était arrivé . . . la dernière fois . . .
[Took me awhile, but eventually I realized I didn't get my period in a long time. I was totally freaked out. The last time this happened . . . last time . . .]

ANCESTOR: Gii-gimoodiwag.
[She was stolen.]

Awe nitam abinoojiiyens Rhonda.
[That first baby is Rhonda.]

TANYA: Rhonda.

ANCESTOR: Tanya awe abinoojii ningii-bi-miinigoo. Gimaamaayens Mags.
[That child was taken to me, Tanya. Your Auntie Mags.]

TRIP: Margaret. Ramona Ohna. Tanya. Rhonda. Lisa.

ANCESTOR: Ningii-wiindamaagoyan egii-niboyan.
[They told us you died.]

TANYA: J'me suis sauvée pour m'en aller à la ville et suis devenue invisible—ils pouvaient pas. Me. Trouver. J'suis sûre que ma fille, ma bébé fille, s'est fait vendre à un petit couple de blancs parce qu'elle ressemblait tellement au petit blanc qui a forcé la porte de mon propre corps. Encore et encore. Je l'ai cherchée partout. Je la voyais partout sans jamais pouvoir la tenir, même pas une fois. Et je me sentais comme morte.
[I ran to the city and became invisible—they could. Not. Find me. Bet my girl, my baby girl, got sold to some white couple 'cause she came out looking so much like the white boy who forced me outside my own body. Again and again. Looked for her everywhere. Seeing her everywhere and never holding her, not once. And I felt like I was dead.]

Puis un loup / est venu.
[Then a wolf / came along.]

TRIP: Then a wolf came along.

TANYA: Pis il m'a dit qu'il pouvait me montrer le chemin. Alors je l'ai suivi.
[And he said he'd show me the way. And I followed.]

TRIP: Because you were starved.

TANYA: Tout le long jusqu'au Gold Star Motor Inn. Il m'a mis dans une chambre spéciale pour les grandes filles loin de chez elles. Avec un lit spécial avec bon nombre de visiteurs et une porte tournante. Et les visiteurs forçaient la porte de mon corps encore et encore. L'un après l'autre après l'autre.
[All the way to the Gold Star Motor Inn. He put me in a special room for big girls far from home. With a special bed with lots of visitors and a rotating door. And the visitors forced me out of my body again and again. One after another after another.]

ANCESTOR: Gaa-baazhkiziged anang.
[Shooting star.]

TANYA: Puis un jour. Deux loups sont venus. Deux loups sur leurs pattes arrières.
[Then one day, two wolves came to visit. Two wolves on hind legs.]

TRIP: Two wolves in human skins.

TANYA: Pis ils m'ont envoyée vraiment très loin de mon propre corps. Ils ont pris ma vie et m'ont jetée sur mon propre lit.
[And they sent me very far away from myself. They picked up my life and threw me over in my own bed.]

TRIP: Rusty-barbed-wire bed.

TANYA: Barbelé et ensanglanté. Jusqu'à ce qu'ils croient que la vie m'avait quittée pour toujours.
[Barbed and bloodied. Until they thought my life was gone for good.]

ANCESTOR: Gaawiin dash gii-maajiiyaamagasinoon.
[But it wasn't gone.]

TANYA: Mais c'était juste ici (juste au-dessus de la tête).
[It was just right there (just overhead).]

City lights blur and dance like northern lights.

TRIP: Watching.

ANCESTOR: Bii'o.
[Waiting.]

TANYA: Pour le corps d'être à nouveau en lieu sûr.
[For the body to be safe again.]

TRIP: And then they wrapped that sheet up tight.

TANYA: Et ils sont sortis direct, par la porte d'en avant.
[And walked right out the front door]

ANCESTOR: Imaa onji Ozaawaa Zhooniyaa Anang Gabeshiwigamig.
[Of the Gold Star Motor Inn.]

TRIP: And dropped that body into the back seat.

TANYA: L'esprit à la suite à la suite.
[Spirit follows follows.]

ANCESTOR: Amii zhigo gii-bimibizonigewag.
[And they drove.]

TANYA: À la suite à la suite.
[Follow follow.]

TRIP: Until no light shone on what they'd done.

ANCESTOR: Akwajiing nakake odenaang.
[Outside the city.]

TANYA: Où le silence touche la terre.
[Where silence touches land.]

TRIP: That blue Impala / parked.

TANYA: Ne s'avouerait jamais.
[Would never come clean.]

ANCESTOR: Miskwiiwan zhigo gaazhaa.
[Bloodied and barbed]

TANYA: Et ils ne savaient pas que je respirais. Juste à peine.
[And they did not know that I was breathing. Just barely.]

TRIP: Breathing.

TANYA: J'inspire.
[In.]

TRIP: Out.

ANCESTOR: Bawaajigewin.
[Dreaming.]

TRIP: In.

TANYA: J'expire. Et ces loups se sont rendus compte que les loups ne conduisent pas, ils tuent et festoient et courent. Donc ils ont couru, lâchant leur hurlement, jusque dans les bois. Et leur hurlement a fait trembler la terre. Et mon corps s'est endormi avec mon esprit
[And out. And those wolves realized that wolves don't drive, they kill and feast and run. And they had had their fill. So they ran off, howling, into the woods. And their howling shook the earth. And my body slept as my spirit—]

TRIP: —watched and waited—

ANCESTOR: —owiiyaawin miinawaa ji-naagachitoowaad.
[—for the body to be safe again.]

TANYA: La terre, dans son silence brimé, a chanté pour moi.
[The earth, in her shaken silence, sang to me.]

Distant singing in vocables.

C'est trop dur d'être une fille autochtone—
[It's too hard to be an Indigenous girl—]

TRIP: It's too hard to be an Indigenous girl—

ANCESTOR: Onzaam zanagan ji-Anishinaabewi-ikwezensiyan—
[It's too hard to be an Indigenous girl—]

TANYA: —qui est tombée sur terre—
[—who fell to earth—]

TRIP: —and keeps on getting pushed over—

ANCESTOR: —miinawaa zhigo miinawaa—
[—and over and over—]

TANYA: —et qui continue à se relever—
[—to keep getting up—]

ANCESTOR: —miinawaa zhigo miinawaa—
[—over and over—]

TRIP: —and over.

TANYA: Et mon esprit est revenu dans mon corps et je me suis secouée. Secoué le sang de mes yeux, de mes dents. Le sang et les os dépris de la banquette arrière. J'ai saisi le volant et j'ai roulé loin de tous les

motels. Et cette Impala que j'avais gagnée. Elle m'a abritée comme je t'ai abritée.
[And spirit returned to my body and I shook. The blood from my eyes, from my teeth. Blood and bones unstuck from the back seat. And I grabbed that wheel and I motored right far from every motor inn. And that Impala I had earned, it housed me as I housed you.]

TRIP: So, it took you a while.

ANCESTOR: Amii sago, ginwenzh igo gi-gii-izhise.
[So, it took you a while.]

TANYA: Ça m'avait pris du temps, t'sais, mais éventuellement j'ai bien vu que j'avais pas mes règles depuis longtemps. J'étais totalement effrayée. La dernière fois que c'était arrivé . . . la dernière fois . . .
[So, it took me a while, but eventually I realized I didn't get my period in a long time. I was totally freaked out. The last time this happened . . . last time . . .]

TRIP: But this time—

TANYA: Je savais qu'elle était une louve. Une louve humaine qui aurait de l'amour et de la douceur. Je serai en sécurité et purifiée. Alors elle devait rester un secret. J'allais être une maman louve et ça allait être la meilleure chose pour moi.
[I knew she was a wolf. A human wolf who would have love and softness. She would make me safe and clean. So she had to stay a secret. I was going to be a wolf mom and it was gonna be my best thing.]

TRIP: And so you drove.

TANYA: Donc j'ai conduit, conduit, conduit. Pour aller voir mon cousin et lui dire que j'allais être okay, pour le lui dire comme ça j'allais savoir que je le serais, mais pas pour lui dire à propos de mon bébé louve, parce qu'elle était un secret sacré pis lui c'était Dis-leur Tyler.

Elle est restée en moi et on est resté dans l'Impala bleue et on l'a remplie un peu plus jour après jour. Pis un jour j'ai senti qu'elle arrivait. *[And drove and drove and drove. To see my cousin and tell him I was going to be okay, to tell him so that I knew I would be, but not tell him about my baby wolf, because she was a sacred secret and he is Tell-all Tyler. She stayed in me and we stayed in the blue Impala and we filled it more and more each day. And then I felt her coming.]*

6. FRACKING / GAA-DAAZHKISEG / FRACTURATION

TRIP: So you drove and drove.

ANCESTOR: Apii gaagii-izhiseg ji-gibichiiyan.
[Until you had to stop.]

TANYA: Là où il y avait personne à voir
Et je pouvais la sentir s'en venir du plus profond de moi.
[Where there was nobody to see
And I could feel her coming from the centre of me]

TRIP: In the back, again, of the blue Impala.

TANYA: Mon corps s'est brisé pour s'ouvrir.
[My self broke open.]

ANCESTOR: Michi-babagidinaamon. Bigo gegoo izhiseg michi-babagidinaamon.
Wiikonaamon.
Bagidinaamon.
Mii-gwayak.
Wiikonaamon.
Bagidinaamon.
Mii-iinzhi.
Ga'an gaye giga-biibaagisiimin. Ga'an awiya ji-gendang.
Amii gichi-wiikonaamon nindikwezensim. Haawn daga sa.
[Just keep breathing. No matter what happens, just breathe.
In.
Out.

Good.
In.
Out.
That's it.
And we won't scream. No one can know.
Big breath in please now, my girl. C'mon!]

TANYA: Et tu es arrivée.
[And you arrived.]

ANCESTOR: Amii zhigo gigii-dagoshin.
[And you arrived.]

TRIP: Me.

ANCESTOR: Zhigo opanan gigii-ayaanan.
[And you had lungs.]

TANYA: Et un cœur.
[And heart.]

ANCESTOR: Zhigo nagamon.
[And song.]

TRIP: My relations.

TANYA: On a veillé l'une sur l'autre.
Et je t'ai nourrie en masse.
Et quand j'avais besoin de me nourrir, pour mieux te nourrir, je t'emmaillotais et te cachais tout au fond à l'arrière de l'Impala où tout a commencé pour toi. Et je conduisais vers la nourriture pendant que tu dormais. Je me faufilais parmi les humains avec mon secret sacré bien blottie contre le plancher de la banquette arrière. En sécurité.
[And we kept each other.
And I fed you strong.

And when I needed feeding, to keep feeding you, I bundled you up and tucked you neat down deep in the Impala where you began. And I drove to food as you slept. Sneaking around among the humans with my sacred secret snugged up tight on the floor of the back seat. Safe.]

ANCESTOR: Amii-aabiding giizhigan.
[And then one day.]

TRIP: The wolves could smell the secret.

ANCESTOR: Gii-izhimaagozi.
[Smelled.]

TANYA: Ils ont volé l'Impala bleue.
[They stole that blue Impala.]

ANCESTOR: Zhigo gimooj biinja'ii gaa-gazhkibijigaazod manidoo-miinigoowiziwin.
[And the sacred secret snugged inside.]

> *The sound of two car doors slamming closed, an old car chugging to life and screeching away.*

TANYA: Il faut que je trouve mon sac à main. Si je le trouve, j'aurai mes clés et ma voiture n'ira pas bien loin sans mes clés, donc elles sont sûrement dans mon sac à main. Et si j'ai mon sac à main la voiture peut pas partir bien loin. Elle peut pas partir bien loin. Tu as vu mon sac ? Tu as vu mon sac ?
[I have to find my purse. If I find my purse, I'll have my keys, and my car won't go without my keys, so they must be in my purse. And if I have my purse the car can't be gone. It can't be gone. Have you seen my purse? Have you seen my purse?]

TRIP: You have it.

TANYA: Ah oui.
[Right.]

TRIP unties the bundle she's had secured to her chest and stomach. She sets it down among the safety of the travois.

TRIP: And that blue Impala screeched. And the sacred secret snugged inside—she sang.

Voices beyond sound: a soaring scream.

ANCESTOR: Ga'an gaye ma'iingani-nagamon gii-nagamosii.
[And she didn't sing a wolf song.]

TRIP: She sang the woman song.

ANCESTOR: Amii ma'iinganag gii-ma'iinganiwiwag.
[And the wolves got wolf-y.]

TRIP: And when they got to a bridge—

TANYA: Non.

ANCESTOR: Zhigo gaa-dagoshinowaad aazhoganing—
[And when they got to a bridge—]

TRIP: —they chucked that sacred secret over—

TANYA: NON!

ANCESTOR: —anaamibiing.
[—under the water.]

TRIP: And the second I hit that water, I flew.

And those wolves drop down on all fours and run around the side of that bridge and chase me all the way down the river, wishing they had seen that I was a fish they coulda eaten up whole.
And I look at them as I swim like flying, my human eyes and woman heart telling them:

Both simultaneously in English:

TANYA: Fuck you all.

TRIP: Damn you all

Silence.

Except this story is a boat.

ANCESTOR: —zhigo ziibi—
[—and a river—]

TANYA: À la fois.
[—all at once.]

ANCESTOR: Amii nibiin gii-ishpisemaganoon, gii-ishpisemaganoon.
[And the waters rose and rose.]

TRIP: And we are women driving that boat.

TANYA: Et nous étions des bébés filles en train d'écrire cette histoire.
[And we were baby girls writing that story.]

TRIP: And we were baby girls rising that story.

ANCESTOR: Zhigo giinawind gimaamaayensimin.
[And we are aunties.]

TANYA: Et des mères
[And moms.]

TRIP: And daughters.
And we are found.

TRIP moves her focus to the bundle.
With her family leading, they go to the bundle.
With their help, TRIP opens the bundle to reveal tiny human bones.

ANCESTOR: Awenensh awe abinoojii, giishpin gegaa bagosiwenimowin.
[And what is a child, if not hope?]

Water rushes.

All three simultaneously:

TRIP: Just keep breathing. No matter what happens, just breathe.

ANCESTOR: Michi-babagidinaamon. Bigo gegoo izhiseg michi-bapagidinaamon.

TANYA: Prends juste une grande respiration. Quoiqu'il arrive, prends juste une grande respiration.

End of play.

Tara Beagan is a proud Ntlaka'pamux and Irish "Canadian" halfbreed. She is cofounder/director of ARTICLE 11 with Andy Moro. A11 has worked in Aotearoa, Australia, and Edinburgh. Beagan has served as artistic director, community liaison, and co-artistic associate of Native Earth Performing Arts. Residencies include Cahoots, NEPA, the National Arts Centre, Berton House, Prairie Theatre Exchange, Banff Playwrights Lab, and, in 2024, New Harlem Productions. Nine of her thirty-seven plays are published, and two have received Dora Mavor Moore Award nominations, with one win. In 2020, *Honour Beat* won the Gwen Pharis Ringwood Award. Beagan is also an award-nominated actor and director. She is the 2020 laureate of the Siminovitch Prize.